Behold, I will stand before thee *there*
upon the rock of Horeb . . . .

Exodus 17:6

(Lower Falls of the Yellowstone River:
Courtesy Union Pacific Railroad)

Th... ...good!

V. R. Edman

Nahum 1/7

THEN and THERE!

The Touch of the Eternal Upon Human Hearts

by

V. RAYMOND EDMAN
Chancellor, Wheaton College,
Wheaton, Illinois

ZONDERVAN PUBLISHING HOUSE
GRAND RAPIDS, MICHIGAN

1682

Dedication

To stalwarts in the faith of our Lord Jesus Christ,
fellow servants in Wheaton College who share with
me the burdens and blessings of administration:

Hudson T. Armerding   *Richard F. Gross*
Edward A. Cording   *Jean R. Kline*
Enock C. Dyrness   *David L. Roberts*
John H. Fadenrecht   *Charles W. Schoenherr*
Harold G. Faulkner   *Merrill C. Tenney*
Robert Golter   *Evan D. Welsh*
                                  Howard W. White

Often they have strengthened my heart and hand
in God's glad service.

      ❋   ❋   ❋   ❋   ❋

Rowena Planck Carr edited the manuscript with
diligence and delight. Dolores Lassen and Marjorie
Scoggins did the typing. To them my heartiest
appreciation.

V. RAYMOND EDMAN

"Westgate"
Wheaton College

O God of Bethel

O God of Bethel! by whose hand
   Thy people still are fed,
Who through this weary pilgrimage
   Hast all our fathers led:

Our vows, our prayers, we now present
   Before Thy throne of grace;
God of our fathers, be the God
   Of their succeeding race!

Through each perplexing path of life
   Our wandering footsteps guide:
Give us each day our daily bread,
   And raiment fit provide.

Oh, spread Thy covering wings around
   Till all our wanderings cease,
And at our Father's love abode
   Our souls arrive in peace.

Such blessings from Thy gracious hand
   Our humble prayers implore,
And thou shalt be our chosen God
   And portion evermore.

— PHILIP DODDRIDGE

Introduction

Then and *there* are really very small words, just four and five letters apiece, but they can be very substantial and meaningful.

In the Bible, as elsewhere, these two little adverbs can be merely routine and commonplace; sometimes they can indicate a situation that is extraordinarily critical. They are primarily adverbs of time and place to indicate when and where something happened. We combine the concepts of when and then; also, if and then. We associate where with there, and sometimes with then itself to give emphasis by saying, "Then and there!"

The Bible has frequent use for both adverbs. To be sure they are frequently merely an indication of time and place. Sometimes, however, the emphasis seems to hinge on the *then* because it was just at that time that something significant transpired; or it was *there*, in that place, where it happened. We can meet God at some *then* or *there* as we read His Word, and all of life can be different because of that meeting.

My heart has often paused at one of these little adverbs of time or place to reflect upon the relationship implicit in them. I have sought to sit alongside Jeremiah and understand why he wrote, *"Then* I knew why this was the word of the Lord" (32:8). I have sought to stand with Joshua as he received instruction and encouragement from the Most High who said: "This book of the law shall not depart out of thy mouth; but thou shalt meditate therein day and night, that thou mayest observe to do according to all that is written therein: for *then* thou shalt make thy way prosperous, and *then* thou shalt have good success" (1:8). I have imagined myself walking with Elijah to his hideaway on the brook Cherith and pondered the promised provision of the Almighty: "I have commanded the ravens to feed thee *there*" (I Kings 17:4).

Do I understand the lessons indicated in *then* and *there*, and do I apply these principles to my own life? All Scripture is indeed inspired of God and all of it is profitable. Am I also a doer of the Word as well as a reader of it?

Pause with me now at some *then* and *there* and let us spend time before the Lord in tenderness of heart and teachableness of spirit.

Then can be a moment of decision, with full awareness of its significance, so that we count the cost of discipleship before putting the hand to the plow. *There* can be a place of destiny, a meeting with the Most High, a hush of heart, a bowing of the will, a complete confidence in Him and commitment to Him, with assurance that prayer will be answered. *Then* there can be an arising to go an unknown way in obedience to the Faithful One who knows the end from the beginning; and there can be no turning back. *There* is a sort of "bench mark" of blessing to be remembered always, an established basis from which to measure the mercies of the Measureless One in days to come, just as the surveyor establishes his bench mark showing latitude, longitude and altitude. All future measurements in that area are based upon the bench mark.

God meets the trusting soul *then* and *there* in time and at some place, thus giving a foretaste now of the timelessness and spacelessness of an eternity with Him whose Word is forever established in heaven.

Table of Contents

THEN and THERE!

ACKNOWLEDGMENTS

The scenic photos in this book were provided by the Union Pacific Railroad Company and used with its permission.

Give to the Winds Thy Fears

Give to the winds thy fears;
  Hope, and be undismayed:
God hears thy sighs, and counts thy tears;
  God shall lift up thy head.

Through waves, and clouds, and storms,
  He gently clears thy way;
Wait thou His time; so shall the night
  Soon end in joyous day.

He everywhere hath sway,
  And all things serve His might;
His every act pure blessing is,
  His path unsullied light.

Leave to His sovereign sway
  To choose and to command;
With wonder fill'd thou then shalt own
  How wise, how strong His hand.

Thou comprehend'st Him not;
  Yet earth and heaven tell
God sits as Sovereign on His throne —
  He ruleth all things well.

— P. GERHARDT
(translated by John Wesley)

1

THERE will your heart be also

Lay not up for yourselves treasures upon earth, where moth and rust doth corrupt, and where thieves break through and steal: but lay up for yourselves treasures in heaven, where neither moth nor rust doth corrupt, and where thieves do not break through nor steal: for where your treasure is, there will your heart be also. . . .

No man can serve two masters: for either he will hate the one, and love the other; or else he will hold to the one, and despise the other. Ye cannot serve God and mammon. Therefore I say unto you, Take no thought for your life, what ye shall eat, or what ye shall drink; nor yet for your body, what ye shall put on. Is not the life more than meat, and the body than raiment? Behold the fowls of the air: for they sow not, neither do they reap, nor gather into barns; yet your heavenly Father feedeth them. Are ye not much better than they? Which of you by taking thought can add one cubit unto his stature? And why take ye thought for raiment? Consider the lilies of the field, how they grow; they toil not, neither do they spin: and yet I say unto you, that even Solomon in all his glory was not arrayed like one of these. Wherefore, if God so clothe the grass of the field, which today is, and tomorrow is cast into the oven, shall he not much more clothe you, O ye of little faith? Therefore take no thought, saying, What shall we eat? or, What shall we drink? or, Wherewithal shall we be clothed? (for after all these things do the Gentiles seek:) for your heavenly Father knoweth that ye have need of all these things. But seek ye first the kingdom of God, and his righteousness; and all these things shall be added unto you. Take therefore no thought for

15

the morrow: for the morrow shall take thought for the things of itself. Sufficient unto the day is the evil thereof. —Matthew 6:19-21, 24-34

For where your treasure is, *there* will your heart be also.
—Matthew 6:21

IN *Pilgrim's Progress*, John Bunyan gave several illustrations of this truth that one's heart is inextricably attached to one's treasure. Particularly pertinent is the picture of Passion and Patience. These two lads were seated at a table in the House of the Interpreter. Pilgrim saw a man pour a bag of jewels and coins on the table. Passion greedily took all for himself while Patience looked on with equanimity and forbearance. Strange to say, in a brief time Passion was poverty-stricken, and greedily cried for more treasure.

"The things which are seen are temporal, but the things which are not seen are eternal," declare the Scriptures (II Corinthians 4:18). One's concept of life will determine one's values. Jesus urges the wisdom of the heavenly viewpoint, setting one's heart and hand to the things that are eternal, as Paul later admonishes those who have passed from spiritual death to new life in Christ Jesus, saying: "Seek those things which are above, where Christ sitteth on the right hand of God," and, "Set your affection on things above, not on things on the earth" (Colossians 3:1, 2). There are spiritual values far more lasting and satisfying than any earthly treasures or achievements of the present time.

Years ago, two old grads met at a Dartmouth dinner in New York City. They had not seen each other for more than forty years. One inquired: "Will, when we were in school you spoke of being a missionary. Your desire has been accomplished. Occasionally I have heard about your pioneer work in South America, the sacrifices you have made, the death of two of your sons in the tropics. Looking back at it all now, how does it seem to you?"

The missionary replied thoughtfully and earnestly, "George, if I had it to do over again I would do exactly what I have done."

Turning to the group, his friend explained, "Fellows, is that not a wonderful thing to say!"

Then the missionary said, "When we were in college, George, you occasionally spoke of your plans: law school after Dartmouth,

16

law practice, election to the state legislature, then to Congress. You have had a long and distinguished career in the service of our country. I have been delighted to see the many honors you have received. With life's goals best accomplished, how does it seem to you?"

"It is all a sucked-out living!" was the astonishing reply.

Life's honors and achievements are only dust and ashes if they are accomplished for ourselves alone. They have constituted our treasure and have had our heart, but there is little genuine or lasting satisfaction in that.

The Saviour explained: "Ye cannot serve God and mammon." One can have both God and gold, but he can serve only one of the two. If he has riches and reveres God so that the Lord Jesus is the pre-eminent one in his life, he can be a faithful steward of the good things God has entrusted to him. If gold is his god, however, he cannot be a true servant of the true and living God.

The Scriptures do not commend poverty as a virtue in itself. The poor are objects of His concern and compassion. Poverty, however, can be the result of our own negligence and indolence. Notice what Solomon observed: "I went by the field of the slothful, and by the vineyard of the man void of understanding; and, lo, it was all grown over with thorns, and nettles had covered the face thereof, and the stone wall thereof was broken down. Then I saw, and considered it well: I looked upon it, and received instruction. Yet a little sleep, a little slumber, a little folding of the hands to sleep: so shall thy poverty come as one that travelleth; and thy want as an armed man" (Proverbs 24:30-34). The last verse may seem a little confusing in the Authorized Translation. The Berkeley Version reads: "And your poverty will come upon you as a bandit, your want like an unyielding warrior."

God can use any person, poor or rich in this world, who is wholly dedicated to Him. Abraham was undoubtedly one of the wealthiest men of his day and he was a "friend of God." There were women of means who helped the Saviour and who "ministered unto Him of their substance" (Luke 8:2, 3). Joseph of Arimathaea was a rich man who boldly went to Pilate to ask that the body of the Lord Jesus be buried in his grave (Matthew 27:

17

57-61; Mark 15:42-46—thus fulfilling the prophecy of Isaiah 53:9 that the Lord Jesus should be "with the rich in His death").

God's Word does not commend poverty or wealth, but it does caution those who have much of this world's goods: "Charge them that are rich in this world, that they be not highminded, nor trust in uncertain riches, but in the living God, who giveth us richly all things to enjoy; that they do good, that they be rich in good works, ready to distribute, willing to communicate; laying up in store for themselves a good foundation against the time to come, that they may lay hold on eternal life" (I Timothy 6: 17-19). This teaching is based upon the observation made earlier in that same chapter: "But godliness with contentment is great gain. For we brought nothing into this world, and it is certain we can carry nothing out. And having food and raiment let us be therewith content. But they that will be rich fall into temptation and a snare, and into many foolish and hurtful lusts, which drown men in destruction and perdition. For the love of money is the root of all evil: which while some coveted after, they have erred from the faith, and pierced themselves through with many sorrows" (I Timothy 6:6-10).

One may have little or much in this world but each must choose for himself to serve God or mammon. The location of the treasure will determine the desire of the heart. The rich young ruler became deeply exercised as to his eternal welfare and ran to the Lord Jesus for help, only to turn away sadly, "for he had great possessions" (Mark 10:17-22). I doubt that Demas had much, but he abandoned the Apostle Paul and turned away from the ministry of the Gospel, "having loved this present world" (II Timothy 4:10). I know wealthy men and women who love God supremely and who are good stewards of all that has been entrusted to them, and I have known poor men who served mammon and disdained the Most High. The basic problem is *where* your treasure is for *there* will your heart be also.

18

2

THEN sang Moses

Then sang Moses and the children of Israel this song unto the Lord, and spake, saying, I will sing unto the LORD, for he hath triumphed gloriously; the horse and his rider hath he thrown into the sea. The LORD is my strength and song, and he is become my salvation; he is my God, and I will prepare him an habitation; my father's God, and I will exalt him. The LORD is a man of war: the LORD is his name. Pharaoh's chariots and his host hath he cast into the sea: his chosen captains also are drowned in the Red Sea. The depths have covered them: they sank into the bottom as a stone. Thy right hand, O LORD, is become glorious in power: thy right hand, O LORD, hath dashed in pieces the enemy. And in the greatness of thine excellency thou hast overthrown them that rose up against thee: thou sentest forth thy wrath, which consumed them as stubble. And with the blast of thy nostrils the waters were gathered together, the floods stood upright as an heap, and the depths were congealed in the heart of the sea. The enemy said, I will pursue, I will overtake, I will divide the spoil; my lust shall be satified upon them; I will draw my sword, my hand shall destroy them. Thou didst blow with thy wind, the sea covered them: they sank as lead in the mighty waters. Who is like unto thee, O LORD, among the gods? who is like thee, glorious in holiness, fearful in praises, doing wonders? Thou stretchedst out thy right hand, the earth swallowed them. Thou in thy mercy hast led forth the people which thou hast redeemed: thou hast guided them in thy strength unto thy holy habitation. — Exodus 15:1-13

Then sang Moses and the children of Israel this song unto the Lord . . . — Exodus 15:1

THE Israelites had good reason for their singing. The bondage in Egypt and the long years of bitter trials were now behind them. On the night of the Passover when the first-born of Egypt were slain, they had been set free to return to the land of their fathers. With rejoicing they had begun their journey and had bright prospects of soon being out of Egypt and into the Promised Land. The respite had been brief, however, for no sooner had they left than their erstwhile tyrant, the Pharaoh of Egypt, planned their recapture. With increasing bewilderment they observed the pursuit of the Egyptian army, against which they had no defense.

They had been assured by Moses that God was leading them by the right way, not by the shortest way which was through the land of the Philistines, but by the "way of the wilderness of the Red sea" (Exodus 13:17, 18). Obediently they had made their camp by the shores of the sea, only to find themselves hemmed in between it and the Egyptians. With reason they cried to the Lord and to Moses, saying,

> Because there were no graves in Egypt, hast thou taken us away to die in the wilderness? wherefore hast thou dealt thus with us, to carry us forth out of Egypt? Is not this the word that we did tell thee in Egypt, saying, Let us alone, that we may serve the Egyptians? For it had been better for us to serve the Egyptians, than that we should die in the wilderness (Exodus 14:11, 12).

Moses had sought to calm their fears with counsel of assurance, as he said, "Fear ye not, stand still, and see the salvation of the LORD, which he will shew to you to day: for the Egyptians whom ye have seen to day, ye shall see them again no more forever. The LORD shall fight for you, and ye shall hold your peace" (Exodus 14:13, 14). Then they saw Moses stretch forth his hand over the sea, and as the east wind blew the waters parted so that they "went into the midst of the sea upon the dry ground" (14: 21, 22). When everyone was safe on the farther shore, Moses, at God's command, stretched forth his hand again and the sea returned to its place drowning the pursuing Egyptians beneath its waves. "And Israel saw that great work which the LORD did upon the Egyptians: and the people feared the LORD, and believed the LORD, and his servant Moses" (Exodus 14:31).

"Then sang Moses and the children of Israel . . ." (Exodus 15:1).

To be sure they had good reason for singing then; but why could they not have sung the song of faith on the other side of the Red Sea?

Moses could have reminded them of the many promises that God had given him to assure them that the Most High would bring them to their land. From the burning bush the Lord had spoken to Moses, saying,

> I have surely seen the affliction of my people which are in Egypt, and have heard their cry by reason of their taskmasters: for I know their sorrows; and I am come down to deliver them out of the hand of the Egyptians, and to bring them up out of that land unto a good land and a large, unto a land flowing with milk and honey; unto the place of the Canaanites, and the Hittites, and the Amorites, and the Perizzites, and the Hivites, and the Jebusites (Exodus 3:7, 8).

At that time God commanded Moses to

> Go, and gather the elders of Israel together, and say unto them, The LORD God of your fathers, the God of Abraham, of Isaac, and of Jacob, appeared unto me, saying, I have surely visited you, and seen that which is done to you in Egypt: and I have said, I will bring you up out of the affliction of Egypt unto the land of the Canaaanites . . . unto a land flowing with milk and honey (Exodus 3:16, 17).

The judgments upon Egypt had been a confirmation of all that God had told Moses. After nine plagues had been visited upon Egypt the Lord had said to His servant Moses, "Yet will I bring one plague more upon Pharaoh, and upon Egypt; afterwards he will let you go hence: when he shall let you go, he shall surely thrust you out hence altogether" (Exodus 11:1). At the first Passover in Egypt, and the only one in that land, God had told them that they should keep that festival "when the Lord shall bring thee into the land of the Canaanites . . . " (Exodus 13:5). How could promises be more explicit and pertinent? The straightened circumstances of the Israelites between Pharaoh's army to the west and the Red Sea to the east were no indication that God had forgotten to be gracious, that He was not fulfilling all that He had promised. The perplexity and peril were designed by the Almighty to be but a platform upon which He would show His mighty work on behalf of His trusting people.

23

The principle contained in this little adverb, *then,* applies directly to us. In the face of danger, difficulties, distresses, disappointments, disease and even death, can we rest our hearts upon the promises of God and sing the song of faith even before there is any evidence of deliverance? Can we exercise the kind of faith the Apostle Paul did when he stood up for the Lord, when all others had lost hope, and said:

I exhort you to be of good cheer: for there shall be no loss of any man's life among you, but of the ship. For there stood by me this night the angel of God, whose I am, and whom I serve, saying, Fear not, Paul; thou must be brought before Caesar: and, lo, God hath given thee all them that sail with thee. Wherefore, sirs, be of good cheer: for I believe God, that it shall be even as it was told me (Acts 27:22-25)?

There was no apparent difference in the circumstances at that moment, but Paul had the shout of faith, as it were, because of assurance of God's faithfulness to His promise.

How much anxiety and anguish of spirit, how much discouragement and depression we would avoid if we continued to put our trust in God's promises because He Himself made them, and did not concern ourselves with the adverse prospects all about us. He has promised that His presence goes with us, that He will never fail us or forsake us, that He is with us all the days even unto the end of the age. His power is unlimited, and He assures us that His hand is not shortened that it cannot save or His ear heavy that it cannot hear. His plan for our life He will fulfill, and our part is to trust Him even where we cannot trace Him. When we have come to the Red Sea place in life, we are to remember the progress we have made to date and the clear indications of divine guidance thus far; then to believe that He who has led into these dire circumstances will surely deliver us in His time and way.

Job in the depths of depression and darkness was reminded that God, the faithful Creator, "giveth songs in the night" (Job 35:10). David also learned that wonderful truth for, when it seemed that all God's waves and billows had poured over him, he wrote: "Yet the Lord will command his lovingkindness in the daytime, and in the night his song shall be with me, and my prayer unto the God of my life" (Psalm 42:8). The song in the night, the song of the shore of the Red Sea, before there is any indication of God's help, is graphically stated in the conclusion of Psalm 42 —

> Why art thou cast down, O my soul: and why art thou disquieted within me? hope thou in God: for I shall yet praise him, who is the health of my countenance, and my God.

3

THERE He proved them

So Moses brought Israel from the Red sea, and they went out into the wilderness of Shur; and they went three days in the wilderness and found no water.

And when they came to Marah, they could not drink of the waters of Marah, for they were bitter: therefore the name of it was called Marah. And the people murmured against Moses, saying, What shall we drink? And he cried unto the LORD; and the LORD shewed him a tree, which when he had cast into the waters, the waters were made sweet: there he made for them a statute and an ordinance, and there he proved them, and said, If thou wilt diligently hearken to the voice of the LORD thy God, and wilt do that which is right in his sight, and wilt give ear to his commandments, and keep all his statutes, I will put none of these diseases upon thee, which I have brought upon the Egyptians: for I am the LORD that healeth thee.

And they came to Elim, where were twelve wells of water, and threescore and ten palm trees: and they encamped there by the waters.   — Exodus 15:22-27

. . . *there* he proved them.   — Exodus 15:25

GOD puts us to some test so that we ourselves may know how weak we really are; and also to show us His faithfulness and grace. He knows us altogether. We are no surprise to Him. This the Psalmist learned, saying, "O Lord, thou hast searched me,

27

and known me. Thou knowest my downsitting and mine uprising, thou understandest my thought afar off. Thou compassest my path and my lying down, and art acquainted with all my ways" (Psalm 139:1-3). The Most High knows not only our thoughts but even the "intents of the heart," as stated in Hebrews 4:12. Verse 13 continues, "Neither is there any creature that is not manifest in his sight: but all things are naked and opened unto the eyes of him with whom we have to do." To remind us of His complete knowledge regarding us, the Almighty says, "Lift up your eyes on high, and behold who hath created these things, that bringeth out their host by number: he calleth them all by names by the greatness of his might, for that he is strong in power; not one faileth. Why sayest thou, O Jacob, and speakest, O Israel, My way is hid from the LORD, and my judgment is passed over from my God?" (Isaiah 40:26, 27).

The Lord gave many tests to the Israelites that they might realize the depths of their unbelief. When they called for bread, God said to Moses, "Behold I will rain bread from heaven for you; and the people shall go out and gather a certain rate every day, that I may prove them, whether they will walk in my law, or no" (Exodus 16:4). When the Ten Commandments were given at Sinai, Moses assured the people, "Fear not: for God is come to prove you, and that his fear may be before your faces, that ye sin not" (Exodus 20:20). Just before the twelve tribes were to enter the Promised Land God reminded them of the reason for the many testings they had experienced, saying,

> And thou shalt remember all the way which the LORD thy God led thee these forty years in the wilderness, to humble thee, and to prove thee, to know what was in thine heart, whether thou wouldest keep his commandments, or no. And he humbled thee, and suffered thee to hunger, and fed thee with manna, which thou knewest not, neither did thy fathers know; that he might make thee know that man doth not live by bread only, but by every word that proceedeth out of the mouth of the LORD doth man live (Deuteronomy 8:2, 3).

In His grace and goodness God is ever putting His trusting children to the test so that after seeing themselves as they really are they shall clearly see Him. He put Abraham, His friend, to the test, and of Abraham the Scriptures declare (Romans 4: 18-21):

Who against hope believed in hope, that he might become the father of many nations, according to that which was spoken, So shall thy seed be. And being not weak in faith, he considered not his own body now dead, when he was about an hundred years old, neither yet the deadness of Sarah's womb. He staggered not at the promise of God through unbelief; but was strong in faith, giving glory to God; and being fully persuaded that, what he had promised, he was able also to perform.

The experience of the Psalmist, as stated in Psalm 66:8-12, is so similar to our own:

O bless our God, ye people, and make the voice of his praise to be heard: which holdeth our soul in life; and suffereth not our feet to be moved. For thou, O God, hast proved us: thou hast tried us, as silver is tried. Thou broughtest us into the net; thou laidst affliction upon our loins. Thou hast caused men to ride over our heads; we went through fire and through water: but thou broughtest us out into a wealthy place.

The Apostle Paul prayed earnestly that the Lord would deliver him from the "thorn in the flesh, the messenger of Satan" which buffeted him. Then it was that he learned that God's grace was sufficient for him, that human strength was made perfect in weakness, and he could testify, "Most gladly therefore will I rather glory in mine infirmities, that the power of Christ may rest upon me. Therefore I take pleasure in infirmities, in reproaches, in necessities, in persecutions, in distresses for Christ's sake: for when I am weak, then am I strong" (II Corinthians 12: 9, 10).

In the Marah experience the Israelites found themselves in great difficulty. There was no water for that vast multitude and for the flocks and herds which were a substantial part of their food supply. The desert seemed to mock them and to say that God had failed them. It was, however, they themselves who were failing God because of their unbelief, and not His failing them. Their part was to call upon Him and not to complain, to pray in faith and not to pity themselves, to plead the promises God had made to them. They were to maintain faith in God and not to murmur against their circumstances nor their leader. The real problem for them in that time of proving was to be, Would they fail God in the test? And that principle applies to each one of us in our times of difficulty.

29

God has great pity toward His people. He knew that they needed not only water but also some outward indication of His presence and power so as to encourage their faith. When Moses prayed in behalf of the people, "the Lord shewed him a tree, which when he had cast into the waters, the waters were made sweet . . ." (Exodus 15:25).

Why a tree? As far as we know it had no chemical qualities wherewith to offset the bitterness of the waters of Marah. Why could Moses just not say a word, or at the most extend his rod over the waters, that the springs might be healed?

It seems that there was a twofold purpose in the use of that tree. First, it was something obvious that God used to create and strengthen the faith of the Israelites, and second, it pictured a great spiritual truth. The tree cast into Marah's waters is a beautiful Old Testament type of the cross of our Lord Jesus. It alone is the answer to the deepest need of the soul because it sweetens every bitterness in life. The waters of your Marah and mine the Saviour will heal by His cross.

The Infinite One is unlimited, and His ways are always higher than our ways. He is not bound by any particular procedure in His answer to prayer. When blind Bartimaeus sought earnestly and insistently healing from his blindness, the Saviour said to him: "Go thy way; thy faith hath made thee whole." The record continues: "And immediately he received his sight, and followed Jesus in the way" (Mark 10:42). When the Lord dealt with the man born blind, He put clay upon his eyes and told him: "Go, wash in the pool of Siloam." The record then says, "He went his way therefore, and washed, and came seeing" (John 9:7).

Why the difference in method, just a word to Bartimaeus and a totally different procedure for the other blind man? It seems to me that the difference is in the two men. Bartimaeus came with faith to the Lord and received immediate help. The man in Jerusalem had time to develop faith as slowly he made his way in the darkness to the Pool of Siloam.

God is mindful of us even in our murmurings, and He accommodates Himself to our limitations. His dealings with us are

30

according to our need and to the measure of our faith and understanding. He knows the bitterness of our Marahs, and He is always faithful.

"*There* he made for them a statute and an ordinance, and *there* he proved them." Every time of testing is a divine opportunity for us to learn some new truth from God's Word, to be assured that God's promises do not fail and that His provision is sure. At the place of proving, just where you are, God is also *there.*

All the Way

All the way my Saviour leads me;
   What have I to ask beside?
Can I doubt His tender mercy,
   Who through life has been my Guide?
Heav'nly peace, divinest comfort,
   Here by faith in Him to dwell!
For I know, whate'er befall me,
   Jesus doeth all things well.

All the way my Saviour leads me,
   Cheers each winding path I tread,
Gives me grace for every trial,
   Feeds me with the living bread.
Though my weary steps may falter,
   And my soul athirst may be,
Gushing from the Rock before me,
   Lo! a spring of joy I see.

All the way my Saviour leads me;
   Oh, the fullness of His love!
Perfect rest to me is promised
   In my Father's house above.
When my spirit, clothed immortal,
   Wings its flight to realms of day,
This my song through endless ages —
   Jesus led me all the way!

—FANNY J. CROSBY

4

THERE upon the rock in Horeb

And all the congregation of the children of Israel journeyed from the wilderness of Sin, after their journeys, according to the commandment of the LORD, and pitched in Rephidim: and there was no water for the people to drink. Wherefore the people did chide with Moses, and said, Give us water that we may drink. And Moses said unto them, Why chide ye with me? wherefore do ye tempt the LORD? And the people thirsted there for water; and the people murmured against Moses, and said, Wherefore is this that thou hast brought us up out of Egypt, to kill us and our children and our cattle with thirst? And Moses cried unto the LORD, saying, What shall I do unto this people? they be almost ready to stone me. And the LORD said unto Moses, Go on before the people, and take with thee of the elders of Israel; and thy rod, wherewith thou smotest the river, take in thine hand, and go. Behold, I will stand before thee there upon the rock in Horeb; and thou shalt smite the rock, and there shall come water out of it, that the people may drink. And Moses did so in the sight of the elders of Israel. And he called the name of the place Massah, and Meribah, because of the chiding of the children of Israel, and because they tempted the LORD, saying, Is the LORD among us, or not?   — Exodus 17:1-7

Behold I will stand before thee *there* upon the rock in Horeb . . .
                                    — Exodus 17:6

33

THE account states that "the people thirsted *there* for water; and the people murmured against Moses . . ." It was right there that God would be, just where the need was greatest and the complaining was loudest.

There is divine provision for our every need. The Scriptural teaching on that point is summarized in the experience of the Apostle Paul in Philippians 4:19: "But my God shall supply all your need according to his riches in glory by Christ Jesus." God's people are not to be fainthearted nor fearful. We are not to be like the children of Israel who saw their circumstances but not the Sovereign of the universe, their faithful Creator. They were painfully aware of the desert wastes but were oblivious of the divine Worker. The pillar of cloud by day and the fire by night was ever with them, but they failed to perceive that it was the covenant presence of Him who promised to provide all their need. In their human hopelessness they failed to remember that God was their helper.

The Israelites were rightfully mindful of their children and of their cattle. It could be that they may have been more distressed by the continual crying of the children and the potential loss of their flocks and herds than they were distressed about their own need. It can be that the responsibilities God has given to us weigh more heavily upon us in the hour of grave difficulty than even we ourselves, and as a result we are inclined to complain bitterly because of fear and frustration. It appears that everything we hold dear and necessary will be lost.

For our every *there* of need God is *there* with His unfailing supply. Like the Israelites we have set forth on a pathway of obedience to our Lord. The way has grown harder even to the point of impossibility, and we begin to rationalize: Would it not be better to turn back to our Egypt which we left, for there life was easier than on this straight and narrow way?

When such thoughts crowd in upon us and when others complain, we are to remember Moses. He was beginning to learn God's faithfulness as stated in the New Testament commentary (Hebrews 11:27) — "he endured, as seeing him who is

34

invisible." He saw all that his people saw, but more than that he also saw God. For him there was no turning back to Egypt, only a trusting in God whatever might be the circumstance of the moment.

Like Moses we are to take to the Lord the complaint of others and not to make reply to them. In response to their murmuring, Moses "cried unto the Lord . . ." In a sense, he was rechecking the divine instructions and requesting help of the Most High. In effect he was doing what long afterward the Scriptures admonished, saying, "Let us therefore come boldly unto the throne of grace, that we may obtain mercy, and find grace to help in time of need" (Hebrews 4:16).

Moses took the burden to the Lord just as in other days the Prophet Elijah did when the widow of Zarephath cried to him because of the death of her only son. The prophet made no defense of God's character and compassion; he only said, "Give me thy son" (I Kings 17:19). When others complain, it is not the occasion for us to seek to justify God's ways; just take the matter home to Him.

It was at Meribah that the Israelites murmured, "Is the Lord among us, or not?" It was just there that Moses learned to be silent before the complainers and thus to have a heart so still that he could hear the Lord say, "Behold, I will stand before thee there upon the rock Horeb; and thou shalt smite the rock, and there shall come water out of it that the people may drink" (17:6).

Psalm 95 (vv. 6-9) contains a commentary on this very experience of Moses and the Israelites at Meribah. This is the exhortation:

> O come, let us worship and bow down: let us kneel before the Lord our maker. For he is our God, and we are the people of his pasture, and the sheep of his hand. To day if ye will hear his voice, harden not your heart, as in the provocation, and as in the day of temptation in the wilderness: when your fathers tempted me, proved me, and saw my work.

If we are hurt by the causeless and ceaseless complaining of our critics, then our heart can become so hardened that we do not hear the divine voice of assurance and instruction. The lesson is for us to humble ourselves, to worship and bow down before the Most High and thus to honor Him. We are to judge ourselves and not others, nor are we to justify God to them. Our part is to get out of the way so God can vindicate Himself, and in so doing He vindicates our confidence in Him.

Our part is to trust and obey, and it is God's part to be *there* in His own way and time. The reviling of the crowd may be loud in our ears, and the rock before us may seem to be as flinty and unyielding as ever. What could Moses' rod do to that rock, a mere stick against a mighty stone? For Moses it was not just a matter of rod and rock. How ridiculous they would have been in themselves! But the important matter was that God Himself was there. His ways are always higher than our ways as heaven is higher than the earth.

The divine commentary on the Meribah experience is stated in Psalm 78:15, 16:

> He clave the rocks in the wilderness, and gave them drink as out of the great depths. He brought streams also out of the rock, and caused waters to run down like rivers.

It was not a mere trickle of water that came from the smitten rock, a tiny spring where each in turn might stoop to drink a wee bit for himself. No, the waters ran like great rivers in the desert, ample for all the people, who possibly numbered two million, and also for their numerous flocks and herds.

God is able to supply all our needs, not only for ourselves individually but for those we represent, and for those who complain in their unbelief. God still does the "exceeding abundantly." For every *there*, ours as well as that of others, God is *there* as well. His ear is not heavy so that it cannot hear our prayer. His eye is not dim so that it cannot see our predicament. His hand is not shortened so that it cannot reach out to help us. He is aware of the criticism heaped upon us. He knows there is no visible source of supply for their need and ours. He also knows the heart that is fully trusting Him, and He is right *there* to help in His own time and way.

Like Moses we also are to learn that "he that cometh to God must believe that he is, and that he is a rewarder of them that diligently seek him." We are to learn by experience to "endure as seeing him who is invisible." He will stand there on the appointed place of faith and faithfulness. Believe Him and see for yourself!

5

THEN came Amalek

Then came Amalek, and fought with Israel in Rephidim. And Moses said unto Joshua, Choose us out men, and go out, fight with Amalek: to morrow I will stand on the top of the hill with the rod of God in mine hand. So Joshua did as Moses had said to him and fought with Amalek: and Moses, Aaron, and Hur went up to the top of the hill. And it came to pass, when Moses held up his hand, that Israel prevailed: and when he let down his hand, Amalek prevailed. But Moses' hands were heavy; and they took a stone, and put it under him, and he sat thereon; and Aaron and Hur stayed up his hands, the one on the one side, and the other on the other side; and his hands were steady until the going down of the sun. And Joshua discomfited Amalek and his people with the edge of the sword. And the Lord said unto Moses, Write this for a memorial in a book, and rehearse it in the ears of Joshua: for I will utterly put out the remembrance of Amalek from under heaven. And Moses built an altar, and called the name of it Jehovah-nissi: ("the Lord our banner") For he said, Because the Lord hath sworn that the Lord will have war with Amalek from generation to generation.　　　　— Exodus 17:8-16

Then came Amalek, and fought with Israel in Rephidim.
　　　　　　　　　　　　　　　　　　　　　— Exodus 17:8

THERE is an Amalek in your future!

He is the adversary of mankind, and is vividly described in the Scriptures as "the Enemy," "the god of this world," "the prince of the power of the air," "the dragon that old serpent," "the Devil" and "Satan." He knows just when and where to attack God's people.

Israel soon learned that not all her enemies were in Egypt. Pharaoh was not the only foe they were to face. They may have been under the impression after they had passed through the Red Sea and escaped the Egyptian army that there were no more battles to be fought.

The Red Sea is typical of the experience of the child of God coming out of Egypt (the world) through the new birth into newness of life. At first the Christian life can seem so wonderful that one can gather the impression that all the difficulties and dangers are in the past. Not so for us as it was not the experience of the children of Israel.

There were testings as well as triumphs—the passage through the Red Sea, the bitter waters of Marah made sweet, the rest under the palm trees of Elim, the supply of daily manna; then came the testing of their faith at Rephidim and the supply of water from the flinty rock.

After prayer has been wonderfully answered and God's provision becomes our portion, then we are grateful for the unfailing presence of the Lord with His people. We rejoice in His protection and His power, and are persuaded that never again will we doubt His faithfulness. Then comes Amalek.

The Amalekites were fierce, implacable dwellers of the desert through whose border the Israelites had to pass. Amalek was determined to stop the onward march of Israel. Just so, our enemy is determined that we shall not make further advance in the Christian life. After our delight in God's goodness to us, there comes the discipline of dismay and the possibility of defeat at the hand of the adversary. To be unfamiliar with spiritual warfare is to find ourselves in imminent danger of being driven backward and defeated.

Israel was relatively inexperienced and unprepared for warfare. They had been slaves in Egypt for generations and were without military training or experience. However, they had Moses as their leader, of whom it was said that he was "learned in all the wisdom of the Egyptians, and was mighty in words and in deeds" (Acts 7:22). Jewish tradition declares that Moses was a general in Pharaoh's army before he fled from Egypt at the age of forty. His skill in leading the relatively unorganized Israelites on their long journey would indicate military training and competence. Furthermore, there was Joshua, a young man hitherto unknown, but one who had the potential of a mighty warrior. Moses was the administrator and Joshua the man of action.

The account of the battle against Amalek is very instructive for us in the Christian life. Fearlessly Joshua and his chosen troops faced the foe, and at the same time Moses went to the top of a neighboring hill where he gave himself to prayer. The victory in the valley was more dependent upon the intercession of Moses, the man of God on the hill top, than the intrepidity of Joshua and his soldiers.

Spiritual warfare is alluded to in various portions of Scripture and especially in Ephesians 6:10-18. There the Christian is given specific instruction and strong encouragement:

> Finally, my brethren, be strong in the Lord, and in the power of his might. Put on the whole armour of God, that ye may be able to stand against the wiles of the devil. For we wrestle not against flesh and blood, but against principalities, against powers, against the rulers of the darkness of this world, against spiritual wickedness in high places. Wherefore take unto you the whole armour of God, that ye may be able to withstand in the evil day, and having done all, to stand. Stand therefore, having your loins girt about with truth, and having on the breastplate of righteousness; and your feet shod with the preparation of the gospel of peace; above all, taking the shield of faith, wherewith ye shall be able to quench all the fiery darts of the wicked. And take the helmet of salvation, and the sword of the Spirit, which is the word of God: praying always with all prayer and supplication in the Spirit, and watching thereunto with all perseverance and supplication for all saints.

We need all the armor of God not just part of it. Basic is our persuasion that the truth of God is given to us in the Scriptures, and that we are to put on the righteousness of Christ to cover our hearts. The shield of faith is used as an offensive weapon to ward off all the wicked reviling of the enemy, and our head must have the helmet of God's salvation. We use the sword of the Spirit, the Word of God, as did the Saviour in His conflict with Satan. To each temptation and insinuation of the Wicked One the Lord answered, "It is written . . ."

Note the climax of the armor — the chief weapon — prayer. Without it the remainder of the armor would be insufficient for the Christian warrior. In the contest with Amalek, Israel had both the prevailing prayer of Moses and the armament for Joshua and his troops. The combination is unbeatable.

"Then came Amalek . . ." When he came Israel did not run away. They stood their ground. The Christian is taught explicitly: "Stand therefore!" and in James 4:7, "Resist the devil, and he will flee from you." When under attack we are to check our armor and our orders from the Captain of our salvation, and then face the foe without fear.

In *Pilgrim's Progress*, Bunyan gave graphic description of the fight between Christian and Apollyon. At first Christian was disturbed, and when he checked his armor he found that he had none for his back. Therefore he determined to face the foe, and after dreadful and prolonged conflict he came out as conqueror.

"*Then* came Amalek . . ." To you and to me. We do not relish his coming, but in the name of our conquering Christ we face him fearlessly.

None But Christ Can Satisfy

O Christ, in Thee my soul hath found,
   And found in Thee alone,
The peace, the joy I sought so long,
   The bliss till now unknown.

I sighed for rest and happiness,
   I yearned for them, not Thee;
But while I passed my Saviour by,
   His love laid hold on me.

I tried the broken cisterns, Lord,
   But ah! the waters failed!
E'en as I stooped to drink they'd fled,
   And mocked me as I wailed.

The pleasures lost I sadly mourned,
   But never wept for Thee,
Till grace the sightless eyes received,
   Thy loveliness to see.

Now none but Christ can satisfy,
   None other name for me;
There's love and life and lasting joy,
   Lord Jesus, found in Thee.

— UNKNOWN

6

THEN I (God) will be an enemy

Behold, I send an Angel before thee, to keep thee in the way, and to bring thee into the place which I have prepared. Beware of him, and obey his voice, provoke him not; for he will not pardon your transgressions: for my name is in him. But if thou shalt indeed obey his voice, and do all that I speak; then I will be an enemy unto thine enemies, and an adversary unto thine adversaries. For mine Angel shall go before thee, and bring thee in unto the Amorites, and the Hittites, and the Perizzites, and the Canaanites, the Hivites, and the Jebusites: and I will cut them off. Thou shalt not bow down to their gods, nor serve them, nor do after their works: but thou shalt utterly overthrow them, and quite break down their images. And ye shall serve the LORD your God, and he shall bless thy bread and thy water; and I will take sickness away from the midst of thee.

— Exodus 23:20-25

Then I will be an enemy unto thine enemies, and an adversary unto thine adversaries.　　　　　　　　— Exodus 23:22

"MR. President, I am sure that God is on our side!"

To this spontaneous and perhaps superficial observation, Abraham Lincoln is said to have replied: "I am not concerned as to whether or not God is on our side, but rather that we are on His side."

45

There is the gracious possibility and the wonderful reality of being on God's side by implicit faith in Him and by complete obedience to His revealed will. There is the divine desire of the Almighty on our behalf, as expressed through the prayer of the Apostle Paul, that we

> might be filled with the knowledge of his will in all wisdom and spiritual understanding; that [we] might walk worthy of the Lord unto all pleasing, being fruitful in every good work, and increasing in the knowledge of God; strengthened with all might, according to his glorious power, unto all patience and longsuffering with joyfulness (Colossians 1:9-11).

We are further admonished, in Ephesians 5:15-17, to see then that we "walk circumspectly, not as fools, but as wise, redeeming the time, because the days are evil." And therefore we are not to be unwise "but understanding what the will of the Lord is."

Like Moses, we too face an untrodden way, beset no doubt with many difficulties and dangers and with an adversary who will bitterly and relentlessly oppose our walk with God. The experience of Israel can be very instructive to us. We recall the observation of Romans 15:4 — "For whatsoever things were written aforetime were written for our learning, that we through patience and comfort of the scriptures might have hope." What hope except that what God did in behalf of His ancient people, as recorded in the Bible, He will still do for those who trust Him?

The Almighty gave promise to His people that He was not sending them alone, rather, "Behold I send an Angel before thee . . ." The ministry of angels is often written in the Scriptures but apparently is little understood or appreciated. The patriarchs and prophets of old had frequent angelic visitors to help them, to encourage or rebuke them. The ministry of angels was especially conspicuous at the time of our Lord's coming, with messages to Zacharias, Mary, Joseph and to the shepherds. Our Lord often spoke of angels, and the apostles were made aware of their reality. The Scriptural teaching is summarized in Hebrews 1:14—"Are they not all ministering spirits, sent forth to minister for them who shall be heirs of salvation?" And there is the further exhortation, "Be not forgetful to entertain strangers: for thereby some have entertained angels unawares" (Hebrews 13:2).

46

For the Israelites, and likewise for ourselves, the angelic ministry is to keep us in the way. God knows that the straight and narrow way that leads to life everlasting may become long and arduous, and we may be tempted to turn aside from it. Some bypath may seem to be easier and likewise seem to go in the direction that leads to the City of the great King, whereas in reality it leads to Doubting Castle, the property of Giant Despair. Such was the experience of Christian and Faithful told in *Pilgrim's Progress* by way of warning. It is the purpose of God's angel to keep us in God's way, to keep us going forward and not sitting down by life's roadside, so that we finish life's assignment with gladness.

Furthermore, it is the aim of the angel to bring us into the place God has prepared for us. He does have such a place for each one in the center of His will. That place may have already been made plain to us, or it may be wholly unknown. The important consideration for us is to reach that prepared place.

The pathway to that place may not seem at the moment to be promising nor propitious. The door that opens before us may be a small one, and behind it is an inconspicuous assignment, perhaps something no one else cares to assume. We had expected that God would lead us into a large place and not to this tiny one which appears to be so meaningless. The Israelites expected soon to be brought into the land that flowed with milk and honey, but for many years they were in the desert. Such may be the trial of our faith, but we can count upon the angel of His presence to keep us in His way and to bring us in His time into the place prepared for us.

Over the years I have observed that a little door which we enter in faith and obedience leads to a larger door. The latter we would not find until we have passed through the low portal of a small place. I have further observed that there are those who never reach the place God has prepared for them because they refuse to enter the humble and obscure responsibilities placed before them.

There is the warning that we be sensitive of heart to the guidance of God's angel, that we "obey his voice." The promise follows, "If thou shalt indeed obey his voice, and do all that I speak; then I will be an enemy unto thine enemies, and an adversary unto thine adversaries." In the center of God's will we learn the reality stated in Philippians 1:28 — "And in nothing terrified by your adversaries: which is to them an evident token of perdition, but to you of salvation, and that of God."

Then we begin to appreciate God's promise in Isaiah 54:17 — "No weapon that is formed against thee shall prosper; and every tongue that shall rise against thee in judgment thou shalt condemn. This is the heritage of the servants of the LORD, and their righteousness is of me, saith the LORD." In times of pressure and perplexity we recall the protection promised in Isaiah 41: 10-13 —

> Fear thou not; for I am with thee: be not dismayed; for I am thy God: I will strengthen thee; yea, I will help thee; yea, I will uphold thee with the right hand of my righteousness. Behold, all they that were incensed against thee shall be ashamed and confounded: they shall be as nothing; and they that strive with thee shall perish. Thou shalt seek them, and shalt not find them, even them that contended with thee: they that war against thee shall be as nothing, and as a thing of nought. For I the LORD thy God will hold thy right hand, saying unto thee, Fear not; I will help thee.

Then the Lord will make real to us what He promised to Israel — to bring them into the land (v. 23) and to find His blessing as stated in verse 25, "And ye shall serve the LORD your God, and he shall bless thy bread, and thy water; and I will take sickness away from the midst of thee." All this will not be done in a day, rather, "By little and little I will drive them [our foes] out from before thee, until thou be increased, and inherit the land" (v. 30).

All this: the angel of His presence, the pathway, the prepared place, protection and provision, for those who obey God's voice and do all that He says!

7

The ravens to feed thee THERE

And Elijah the Tishbite, who was of the inhabitants of Gilead, said unto Ahab, As the LORD God of Israel liveth, before whom I stand, there shall not be dew nor rain these years, but according to my word. And the word of the LORD came unto him, saying, Get thee hence, and turn thee eastward, and hide thyself by the brook Cherith, that is before Jordan. And it shall be, that thou shalt drink of the brook; and I have commanded the ravens to feed thee there. So he went and did according unto the word of the LORD: for he went and dwelt by the brook Cherith, that is before Jordan. And the ravens brought him bread and flesh in the morning, and bread and flesh in the evening; and he drank of the brook. — I Kings 17:1-6

I have commanded the ravens to feed thee *there*. — I Kings 17:4

> In the center of God's will I stand;
> There can be no second causes,
> All must come from His dear hand.

THERE is "the center of God's will" for each life. What it is for you and me is something that must be made clear between the Most High and the individual heart. For Elijah the prophet it was, for the time being, a place of complete obscurity beside the brook Cherith. God defined it explicitly as being *there*.

We know little of Elijah's background. He appeared suddenly in the history of Israel during the days of wicked King

Ahab. Without doubt he had been prepared by God during his youth, perhaps even in childhood, so that he could say to the king, "As the Lord God of Israel liveth, before whom I stand . . ." He was God's man for those times, a man utterly dedicated to God, willing for anything that his Lord might ask him to do or say. Because he feared God he was fearless before men. Of a naturally fiery disposition, he became indeed a prophet of fire; but before God he walked in lowly fidelity.

Elijah was an earnest patriot as well as a man of God. His country was in a critical condition because of wickedness and idolatry in high places and low. It must have seemed to the prophet that he was needed more than ever at that time, yet his Lord made plain to him that he was to go to the place of complete obscurity to await God's hour of deliverance for his land.

For Elijah the hideout beside the brook became the secret place of the Most High. In its solitude and silence he learned deep lessons of prayer and patience. The New Testament commentary tells us that he "was a man subject to like passions as we are," but he was mighty in prayer, "and he prayed earnestly that it might not rain: and it rained not on the earth by the space of three years and six months. And he prayed again, and the heaven gave rain, and the earth brought forth her fruit" (James 5:17, 18).

The hidden place beside the brook was also the place of divine supply. God had said that the ravens would feed him *there*. The birds had their instructions as well as did Elijah. Had he not been in God's appointed place it is very doubtful that the ravens would have located him at all. They had no problem of obedience since they were ever ready to do the bidding of their Creator. It is man who has the power of choice to obey God or to ignore Him. As long as Elijah was *there* there was no problem as to divine provision for his need, despite the drought that was destroying the crops. From where the ravens secured their supply of bread and meat is a matter left unknown to us. It was a problem in logistics easily solved by the Lord of heaven and earth.

Elijah might have made objection to the Lord as to His use of ravens. After all they were declared to be "unclean" by the law which stated, "And these are they which ye shall have in abomination among the fowls . . . every raven after his kind . . ." (Leviticus 11:13, 15). The prophet could have said, in substance, "No, Lord, not ravens! Thou knowest that nothing unclean has ever passed my lips. Be pleased to send the food with doves since they are clean birds according to the law of Moses." Elijah might have had the same reaction as did Peter at Joppa when he was told to eat "all manner of four-footed beasts of the earth, and wild beasts, and creeping things, and fowls of the air." To these divine instructions he replied, "Not so, Lord; for I have never eaten anything that is common or unclean" (Acts 10:12, 14).

There is a principle here that deserves our careful attention. One recalls the experience of the late Henry W. Frost, an American businessman who was called into the service of the China Inland Mission in the early days of that movement. Its founder, Hudson Taylor, asked Mr. Frost to become the director of the Mission in North America. As a result Mr. Frost sold his business in New York State, moved to Toronto and established the first receiving home for the missionary candidates en route to the field or returning home on furlough.

Shortly after the home was opened a neighbor stopped in for a brief visit. He was a local politician, neither a Christian nor a man of integrity and good reputation. He inquired about the home and was told of its purpose. As he turned to leave he shook hands with Mr. Frost, and the latter was aware of money being pressed into his palm. The inner reaction was immediate that he should not accept any gift from this person, but he felt the Lord check him in his spirit.

As soon as the visitor was gone Mr. Frost retired to his room to pray. "Dear Lord, Thou knowest this is Thy work to be supported by Thy children, and this man is not one of them. What does this mean?" The Lord's answer was a gracious and very brief question, "And who supplied bread and meat to Elijah?"

The divine principle appears to be that God's work is to be supported by God's people, but, if others on their own initiative offer to help, such aid is to be received with gratitude because the Lord has sent them.

And so Elijah stayed in the place appointed for him by God. Supplied by daily provision in the secret place of the Most High, the prophet also needed steadiness of purpose for, whereas bread and meat were unfailing, the brook dwindled slowly away — and all because of Elijah's own word. Should he not put self-interest and self-preservation first in his life and ask God at least for rain in the area of Cherith so that he would have water to drink? But he quieted his fears on the faithfulness of His God and, until further instructions came, he remained in his *there*.

Is Thy Cruse of Comfort Failing?

Is thy cruse of comfort failing?
   Rise and share it with a friend!
And through all the years of famine
   It shall serve thee to the end.
Love Divine will fill thy storehouse,
   Or thy handful still renew;
Scanty fare for one will often
   Make a royal feast for two.

For the heart grows rich in giving:
   All its wealth is living grain;
Seeds — which mildew in the garner —
   Scattered, fill with gold the plain.
Is thy burden hard and heavy?
   Do thy steps drag wearily?
Help to lift thy brother's burden —
   God will bear both it and thee.

Lost and weary on the mountains,
   Wouldst thou sleep amidst the snow?
Chafe that frozen form beside thee,
   And together both shall glow.
Art thou wounded in life's battle?
   Many stricken round thee moan;
Give to them thy precious ointment,
   And that balm shall heal thine own.

Is thy heart a well left empty?
   None but God its void can fill;
Nothing but a ceaseless fountain
   Can its ceaseless longings still.
Is thy heart a living power?
   Self-entwined, its strength sinks low;
It can only live by loving,
   And by serving love will grow.

                — MRS. E. R. CHARLES

8

The widow woman was THERE

And the word of the LORD came unto him, saying, Arise, get thee to Zarephath, which belongeth to Zidon, and dwell there: behold, I have commanded a widow woman there to sustain thee. So he arose and went to Zarephath. And when he came to the gate of the city, behold, the widow woman was there gathering of sticks: and he called to her, and said, Fetch me, I pray thee, a little water in a vessel, that I may drink. And as she was going to fetch it, he called to her, and said, Bring me, I pray thee, a morsel of bread in thine hand. And she said, As the LORD thy God liveth, I have not a cake, but an handful of meal in a barrel, and a little oil in a cruse: and, behold, I am gathering two sticks, that I may go in and dress it for me and my son, that we may eat it, and die. And Elijah said unto her, Fear not; go and do as thou hast said: but make me thereof a little cake first, and bring it unto me, and after make for thee and for thy son. For thus saith the LORD God of Israel, The barrel of meal shall not waste, neither shall the cruse of oil fail, until the day that the LORD sendeth rain upon the earth. And she went and did according to the saying of Elijah: and she, and he, and her house, did eat many days. And the barrel of meal wasted not, neither did the cruse of oil fail, according to the word of the LORD, which he spake by Elijah.   — I Kings 17:8-16

Behold, the widow woman was *there* gathering of sticks . . .
                    — I Kings 17:10

57

THAT God resists the proud but gives grace to the humble is one of the underlying principles of divine revelation. It is spelled out in detail in I Corinthians 1:26-29 —

> For ye see your calling, brethren, how that not many wise men after the flesh, not many mighty, not many noble, are called: but God hath chosen the foolish things of the world to confound the wise; and God hath chosen the weak things of the world to confound the things which are mighty; and base things of the world, and things which are despised, hath God chosen, yea, and things which are not, to bring to nought things that are: that no flesh should glory in his presence.

This fundamental consideration underlies the account of the prophet Elijah at Zarephath. Clearly he had been led of God to go to the brook Cherith, and there he had remained hidden from the sight of wicked King Ahab and others for a long time. No further word from heaven had come to God's servant until the brook dried up completely because of the protracted drought. God was dealing with Elijah, that prophet of fire, to teach him patience and faithfulness, as well as teaching the nation the reality of divine judgment. By nature Elijah was impetuous, impatient, zealous for God, a patriot who loved his land and also a prophet of the Most High. The discipline of delay at Cherith had been long, and without doubt the prophet was deeply perplexed, perhaps apprehensive, of what might be happening in Israel and in its capital city of Samaria in particular. Would God's Word never come to him again?

Of course it came in God's time and order. One can imagine the inner stir of heart as Elijah was aware that again the Almighty was speaking to him with new instructions. Had the moment come for him to return to king and people with the message of God's wrath against the idolatry and wickedness which were causing drought and famine? Intently Elijah listened to each word. "Arise," God was saying; and very possibly by that time Elijah was already on his feet, with face turned toward his desired homeland and his back to the dried up bed of the brook.

"Get thee to Zarephath which belongeth to Zidon," continued the divine instructions. Zarephath! Not Samaria as he had hoped! Was there to be further delay? Would God's time for judgment upon Baal worship never come?

Such perplexities raced through the mind of the prophet as he stood before God. And Zarephath — a Gentile town in Zidon — Zidonians, enemies of his people! Why Zarephath? Why Zidon? Why not some small village near Samaria? But the lesson of God's provision sent by the ravens had not been misunderstood by Elijah. If his Lord saw best to use birds that were unclean by the Mosaic Law to care for His servant in obscurity, the same Lord could use a stranger, a Gentile, even one of his enemies, to make provision for the prophet until God's hour for Israel should strike.

"And dwell there: behold, I have commanded a widow woman *there* to sustain thee." To dwell there presented no problem to the prophet. Anywhere God would send would be the center of His will. But to a widow! Why not to some wealthy person, to someone who had means whereby to care for God's servant? In Elijah's day, as has always been the case, God looked for some lowly one, inconspicuous and humanly helpless, to whom He could reveal His compassion and His power.

Should the Most High have some special ministry for you, for me, are we so humbled of heart, so insufficient of ourselves that He can use us for His glory? On one occasion a friend said to Hudson Taylor, "When God would found the China Inland Mission, He sought for someone strong and faithful." To this Mr. Taylor replied, "No, I think God looked for someone so weak and insufficient that He could use him in His own way, that He found me."

Obedience was no problem to Elijah. "He arose and went to Zarephath." He probably wondered within himself how he should identify the unknown person to whom God was sending him. Where would she be found? What was her name? "And when he came to the gate of the city, behold, the widow woman was *there* . . . ." Of course she was *there!* She did not know why she had gone to the gate of the city that morning other than that she would gather a few sticks to make a little fire and prepare the last meal for herself and her son. The famine was so great in Zarephath that many were dying, and she had come to that extremity.

It is pointless to surmise what might have transpired had

she decided not to go out to get sticks for the fire. There is no indication in the story that she knew God; but God knew her, and the gracious Holy Spirit directed her thoughts and her steps so that when God's servant came she was *there.*

How did Elijah recognize that this was the one of whom God had spoken? I do not know; but quite possibly he requested a drink of water so as to become acquainted and to make sure that this was the widow of God's appointment. There was some water in Zarephath, and the woman turned herself to do the prophet's bidding. God does no unnecessary miracle. Elijah did not have to smite a rock as did Moses, and thereby astonish the people of Zarephath with a supply of water.

But the widow had no food except "a handful of meal in a barrel and a little oil in a cruse," just enough for one small meal for her son and herself. How could she give first to him? Beyond that, how on earth could she take in a boarder, a stranger and an alien at that?

However, she implicitly obeyed all that Elijah said to her. God had been preparing her heart for just such obedience. Had He not said to His servant, "Behold, I have *commanded* a widow woman there to sustain thee"?

Was it greedy of Elijah to ask the last morsel of food from the widow? No, he knew what God would do, and therefore could say, "The barrel of meal shall not waste, neither shall the cruse of oil fail, until the day that the Lord sendeth rain upon the earth." In substance he was teaching her the truth of Matthew 6:33 — "But seek ye first the kingdom of God, and his righteousness; and all these things shall be added unto you."

Elijah went *there* and dwelt *there.* In the center of God's will there is always God's provision, as we read in Philippians 4:19 — "But my God shall supply all your need according to his riches in glory by Christ Jesus."

9

THEN Jezebel sent a messenger

And Ahab told Jezebel all that Elijah had done, and withal how he had slain all the prophets with the sword. *Then* Jezebel sent a messenger unto Elijah, saying, So let the gods do to me and more also, if I make not thy life as the life of one of them by to morrow about this time. And when he saw that, he arose and went for his life, and came to Beer-sheba, which belongeth to Judah, and left his servant there.

But he himself went a day's journey into the wilderness, and came and sat down under a juniper tree: and he requested for himself that he might die; and said, It is enough; now, O LORD, take away my life; for I am not better than my fathers. And as he lay and slept under a juniper tree, behold, then an angel touched him, and said unto him, Arise and eat. And he looked, and, behold, there was a cake baken on the coals, and a cruse of water at his head. And he did eat and drink, and laid him down again. And the angel of the LORD came again the second time, and touched him, and said, Arise and eat; because the journey is too great for thee. And he arose, and did eat and drink, and went in the strength of that meat forty days and forty nights unto Horeb the mount of God.

And he came thither unto a cave, and lodged there; and behold, the word of the LORD came to him, and he said unto him, What doest thou here, Elijah? And he said, I have been very jealous for the LORD God of hosts: for the children of Israel have forsaken thy covenant, thrown down thine altars, and slain thy prophets with the sword; and I, even I only, am left; and they seek my life, to take it away. — I Kings 19:1-10

63

THERE is nothing quite like the fury of an angry woman. History recounts the callous cruelty of ancient kings and captains but these have been overshadowed by the vindictiveness and viciousness of some women. King Herod was angered by the preaching of John the Baptist who had stated forthrightly that the king was under God's judgment because he had taken his brother's wife. The wrath of the king which imprisoned the preacher was nothing in comparison with the implacable hatred of Herodias who was determined to kill God's prophet and took the first opportunity she had to make sure that his head was delivered to her on a platter.

King Ahab may have seemed to be the acme of wickedness and idolatry, but Jezebel was more wicked than he. Ahab was the son of Omri who "wrought evil in the eyes of the Lord, and did worse than all that were before him" (I Kings 16:25). Ahab outdid his depraved father, for the account continues:

> And Ahab the son of Omri did evil in the sight of the Lord above all that were before him. And it came to pass, as if it had been a light thing for him to walk in the sins of Jeroboam the son of Nebat, that he took to wife Jezebel the daughter of Ethbaal king of the Zidonians, and went and served Baal, and worshipped him. And he reared up an altar for Baal in the house of Baal, which he had built in Samaria. And Ahab made a grove; and Ahab did more to provoke the LORD God of Israel to anger than all the kings of Israel that were before him (I Kings 16:30-33).

But it was Jezebel who was so callously cruel that she could take life without compulsion. She saw to it that as many prophets of the Lord as could be captured were slain, and, had not Obadiah hidden a hundred of them, all would have been killed (I Kings 18:13). To Jezebel it was a light matter to have Naboth falsely accused so that he was stoned to death on the charge of blaspheming God and the king; and thus Naboth's vineyard became Ahab's possession. That story in I Kings 21 concludes with the divine commentary in verse 25: "But there was none like unto Ahab, which did sell himself to work wickedness in the sight of the Lord, whom Jezebel his wife stirred up."

With good reason Elijah feared Jezebel. Who would not?

64

Well, that depends. John the Baptist did not fear King Herod or Herodias, the voluptuous and vindictive queen. He preferred prison and possible death to panic that would bring disrepute upon the truth of God.

After triumph there always comes a time of deep testing. After the fire of God fell upon Carmel's altar and the flood of rains came in answer to prayer, then came the fury of Jezebel. It was after God gave water from the rock at Rephidim that the Amalekites came to drive away the people of God. It was when the Philistines heard that David had been made king that they came to destroy his kingdom (II Samuel 5:17). After Gideon won his great victory with his faithful three hundred men over the Midianites he was tempted to ask for the gold that had been captured, and this became a snare to him (Judges 8:24-27). And it was after Jesus' baptism in the Jordan and the acknowledgment by John and by God the Father, that He was driven into the desert to be tempted by the devil.

Success is always a greater discipline than is failure. Elijah had successfully passed the test of utter obedience to go into the obscurity of Cherith and of Zarephath, and to face the four hundred prophets of Baal along with Ahab and all the royal court. God vindicated the stand of His prophet; but at the pinnacle of Elijah's success came Jezebel.

After intensive activity there comes reaction which may include discouragement, dejection, hopelessness, unbelief. Perhaps Elijah had gone beyond the limits of physical and spiritual strength. After the contest with the priests of Baal and the prayer that had brought fire and rain, need he have run before the king's chariot all the way to Jezreel? Should he have slipped away quietly to some secret place on Mount Carmel, or back to the brook Cherith, or perhaps have gone all the way to Horeb, the mount of God, before going to Samaria? These things we do not know, only that God's servant in the flash of triumph ran directly into Jezebel.

It is easy to criticize the decisions made by another under intense pressure. Most people have 20-20 hindsight, especially in viewing the conduct of another. Had we been in Elijah's place, would we have been willing to fade out of the picture and silently steal away to some hiding place? I doubt it.

After intense effort and the inward exultation of triumph, beware of the downbeat of defeat due to spiritual or physical exhaustion. After the excitement of being in the public eye and the exhilaration of success, take care that excess does not lead to fatigue, fear and frustration. After wonderful answers to prayer and the reality of divine help there will come the counter-attack of the adversary, either as a roaring lion or as an angel of light. It was after King Hezekiah was healed that treacherous Babylonian envoys came to examine his treasures.

Rather than blame some bewildered Elijah, we should have pity and prayer for him. We can learn from him how to stand for the Lord, and what Ephesians 6:13 means: "Wherefore take unto you the whole armour of God, that ye may be able to withstand in the evil day, and having done all, to stand."

Maybe Elijah should have fled from that wicked Jezebel, maybe not. Quite possibly Elijah's ministry had to come to its climactic conclusion, perhaps not. God showed His concern and compassion for His faithful servant by making provision for him on his flight. There is great tenderness in the words of the angel, "Arise and eat; because the journey is too great for thee." Thereafter the prophet was to prepare a successor for himself in the person of young Elisha. There was still some service for Elijah which included the training of Elisha. God's approval of His servant was given with finality in Elijah's ascension into heaven.

The lesson revolves around the *then* of Jezebel's message. *Then* can be the amber light of caution to us after the light has been green for a long time. It means a time of waiting on God, a time to be still and to know that He is God. It is a light for alertness and not for anxiety or fear.

Oh, Give Me Rest From Self

My Saviour, Thou hast offered rest:
    Oh give it, then, to me! —
The rest of ceasing from myself,
    To find my all in Thee.

This cruel self, oh, how it strives
    And works within my breast,
To come between Thee and my soul,
    And keep me back from rest!

How many subtle forms it takes
    Of seeming verity,
As if it were not *safe* to rest,
    And venture all on Thee.

O Lord, I seek a holy rest,
    A victory over sin!
I seek that Thou alone shouldst reign
    O'er all without, within.

In Thy strong hand I lay me down —
    So shall the work be done:
For who can work so wondrously
    As the Almighty One?

Work on, then, Lord, till on my soul
    Eternal light shall break;
And, in Thy likeness perfected,
    I "satisfied" shall wake.

— E. H. HOPKINS

10

THEN shall ye begin to say

And he went through the cities and villages, teaching, and journeying toward Jerusalem. Then said one unto him, Lord, are there few that be saved? And he said unto them,

Strive to enter in at the strait gate: for many, I say unto you, will seek to enter in, and shall not be able. When once the master of the house is risen up, and hath shut to the door, and ye begin to stand without, and to knock at the door, saying, Lord, Lord, open unto us; and he shall answer and say unto you, I know you not whence ye are: Then shall ye begin to say, We have eaten and drunk in thy presence, and thou hast taught in our streets. But he shall say, I tell you, I know you not whence ye are; depart from me, all ye workers of iniquity. There shall be weeping and gnashing of teeth, when ye shall see Abraham, and Isaac, and Jacob, and all the prophets, in the kingdom of God, and you yourselves thrust out. And they shall come from the east, and from the west, and from the north, and from the south, and shall sit down in the kingdom of God. And, behold, there are last which shall be first, and there are first which shall be last.

— Luke 13:22-30

When once the master of the house is risen up, and hath shut to the door . . . *then* shall ye begin to say . . .   — Luke 13:25, 26

IN this incident of our Lord's life and teaching the adverb *then* is used twice. The first time it is merely incidental as it states the occasion on which the inquiry was made by some unnamed individual. He had been listening to the teaching of the Saviour

69

and voiced the question that many of them had, "Are there few that be saved?" It was current opinion among many of Jesus' contemporaries that only a small percentage of mankind would be granted entrance into heaven. This opinion was based on analogy such as the experience of the multitude of Israelites that came out of Egypt, only two of whom (of the adults among them at that time), Caleb and Joshua, actually entered the Promised Land.

Whether the inquiry were one of sincerity or of mere speculation one cannot say, but it is very important to observe that the Saviour did not answer the question directly. To do so might merely have created further idle discussion or even acrimonious controversy among those who were listening to His teaching, or between the inquirer and the Lord Himself. Rather, our Lord replied to all of them present: "Strive to enter in at the strait gate: for many, I say unto you, will seek to enter in, and shall not be able" (Luke 13:24). He thereby placed the responsibility squarely on the individual to make his own decision on the welfare of his soul in the life to come. That responsibility is not a matter of idle speculation, a sort of take-it-or-leave-it as you please.

Our Lord's answer was immediate and graphic. There was no question as to whether or not there is life after death. That existence He affirmed with the utmost clarity and emphasis. He said, "Strive to enter in at the strait gate . . ." (literally, "agonize to enter"); that is, make this your supreme consideration. In no way is our Lord teaching salvation by works. He was stating pointedly that there is but one door into life eternal, that the door is narrow, and that it does open into the Father's house. Elsewhere He explained that He Himself is the door. To the man born blind who had been healed, and to others who stood by, the Saviour declared, "I am the door: by me if any man enter in, he shall be saved" (John 10:9). That same truth He re-emphasized at the Last Supper: "I am the way, the truth, and the life: no man cometh unto the Father, but by me" (John 14:6). The Apostle Peter, after Pentecost, taught plainly, "Neither is there salvation in any other: for there is none other name under heaven given among men, whereby we must be saved" (Acts 4:12).

By striving, agonizing to enter in, the Saviour was teaching that mankind was to turn from the broad way of popular opinion and self-righteous "good works" and make it one's whole desire to enter the door into God's house in God's own way. It is humbling to the human spirit to be saved by faith through grace, apart from any merit of our own. But it is the heart that trusts in God's provision for his redemption that finds God's salvation, and enters the narrow doorway into the family of God.

The door to the Father's house is now open, with invitation for all to enter through saving faith in the Lord Jesus Christ. The Scriptures state urgently, "Behold, now is the accepted time; behold, now is the day of salvation" (II Corinthians 6:2). And the Saviour gives assurance, ". . . him that cometh to me I will in no wise cast out" (John 6:37).

That Scripture greatly troubled John Bunyan. The Tinker of Bedford was greatly exercised about his soul's salvation and assurance of everlasting life. In his careful and earnest reading of the Scriptures he came across John 6:37. At first it filled him with great hope for it said that the Saviour would in no wise cast out those who came to Him. Satan, however, seemed to say, "But you're not coming." "Yes I am coming!" asserted Bunyan fiercely. "You are not coming in the right way," sneered the adversary. "The Word says nothing about how I should come, it only says, Come!" replied the desperate Bunyan. In his characteristic way he added, "Satan took hold of that verse and I did too. He tugged, and I tugged; and by God's help I won out." It was on the basis of John 6:37 that John Bunyan entered the door of salvation and was assured that he was indeed a child of God.

The closing exhortation of the Bible is an invitation to salvation. Revelation 22:17 declares — "And the Spirit and the bride say, Come. And let him that heareth say, Come. And let him that is athirst come. And whosoever will, let him take the water of life freely."

Now is the time to enter, for the time will come when "the master of the house is risen up, and hath shut to the door." Then it will be useless to stand outside, to knock vehemently at the door and to say earnestly, "Lord, Lord, open unto us." He

"shall answer and say unto you, I know you not whence ye are."
No excuses will then be allowed. And the plea, "But I know
about Thee, I know Thy Word which has been taught in my
home, in Sunday school and in church, and in a Christian college," will be ineffectual.

When eternity's door is shut for us, perhaps at our irrevo-
cable decision to reject the Saviour, or at death, or at the Second
Coming of Christ, then it will be pointless to pound upon the
shut door. How foolish to postpone the decision to enter the
door until it is closed forever.

Procrastination is the height of folly. One remembers the
old fable of the medieval king who had as his jester the greatest
fool in his kingdom. One day the king told his jester that he
was going on a long journey from which he would not return.
The court fool replied that the king need have no concern since
he had known about that journey for a long time and surely had
made full provision for it. Sadly the king responded that he had
made no such provision. Thereupon the jester removed his cap
and bells and handed them to his monarch, saying, "If such is
the case, your majesty, you are a greater fool than am I."

11

THEN shall the righteous shine forth

All these things spake Jesus unto the multitude in parables; and without a parable spake he not unto them: that it might be fulfilled which was spoken by the prophet, saying, I will open my mouth in parables; I will utter things which have been kept secret from the foundation of the world. Then Jesus sent the multitude away, and went into the house: and his disciples came unto him, saying, Declare unto us the parable of the tares of the field. He answered and said unto them, He that soweth the good seed is the Son of man; the field is the world; the good seed are the children of the kingdom; but the tares are the children of the wicked one; the enemy that sowed them is the devil; the harvest is the end of the world; and the reapers are the angels. As therefore the tares are gathered and burned in the fire; so shall it be in the end of this world. The Son of man shall send forth his angels, and they shall gather out of his kingdom all things that offend, and them which do iniquity; and shall cast them into a furnace of fire: there shall be wailing and gnashing of teeth. Then shall the righteous shine forth as the sun in the kingdom of their Father. Who hath ears to hear, let him hear.

— Matthew 13:34-43

Then shall the righteous shine forth as the sun in the kingdom of their Father. Who hath ears to hear, let him hear.

— Matthew 13:43

A PARABLE is an illustration designed to teach us some simple truth. The Lord Jesus, the world's greatest teacher, was a master in the art of using parables. He did not go far afield for the illustrations He used; He chose those subjects and objects that were most familiar to His listeners. Furthermore, they are familiar to us today, as they have been in every generation and in every part of the world where the gospel message has been told. The Saviour spoke of the farmer sowing seed in the field, of birds in the trees and seed that fell beside the roads, of the harvest and of fishermen with their nets.

Some parables may seem obscure and even ambiguous to twentieth-century Christians because they have been subjected to various interpretations, as for example the parable of the ten virgins, five of whom were wise and five foolish. But some of the parables were interpreted by the Saviour Himself and such is the case with the parable of the tares in the field.

This parable was of particular interest to the disciples, with the result that they made the inquiry, "Declare unto us the parable of the tares of the field." The Lord Jesus then proceeded to give its explanation in detail. The meaning is so clear and cogent, so searching and startling that we do well to read and reread it with a view of applying it unreservedly to our own lives. Here is indeed a light in which we can see all the world in every age, and it is a mirror into which we can look and see ourselves as well.

The sower is the Son of man, the Saviour Himself. He sows the good seed of the kingdom, namely, "the children of the kingdom." In this parable the seed is not the Word of God itself as was true in the other parable of the sower in which he said, "the seed is the word of God" (Luke 8:11). The sower scatters the children of the kingdom, the sons of God, the men and women of the Word who carry the Gospel to all the world, which is the field. Of them Jesus spoke in His very last word to His disciples before His ascension into heaven, saying, "But ye shall receive power, after that the Holy Ghost is come upon you: and ye shall be witnesses unto me both in Jerusalem, and in all Judaea, and in Samaria, and unto the uttermost part of the earth" (Acts 1:8).

Earlier He had given them the great commission (Matthew 28:18-20):

> All power is given unto me in heaven and in earth. Go ye therefore, and teach all nations, baptizing them in the name of the Father, and of the Son, and of the Holy Ghost: Teaching them to observe all things whatsoever I have commanded you: and, lo, I am with you alway, even unto the end of the world [literally, "the age"].

On another occasion Jesus instructed them that "this gospel of the kingdom shall be preached in all the world for a witness unto all nations; and then shall the end come" (Matthew 24:14).

But in the field there are tares as well as wheat. These are "the children of the wicked one." Their sower is "the devil." The Saviour specifically taught that there is such a personality in the world as the devil, described in the parable itself as "an enemy" (Matthew 13:28). All of us are described as being citizens of his kingdom until we have been delivered from it. The Scriptures declare of believers in Christ that

> you hath he quickened, who were dead in trespasses and sins; wherein in time past ye walked according to the course of this world, according to the prince of the power of the air, the spirit that now worketh in the children of disobedience: among whom also we all had our conversation in times past in the lusts of our flesh, fulfilling the desires of the flesh and of the mind; and were by nature the children of wrath, even as others. But God, who is rich in mercy, for his great love wherewith he loved us, even when we were dead in sins, hath quickened us together with Christ, (by grace ye are saved) . . . (Ephesians 2:1-5).

Of that salvation Colossians 1:13, 14 adds that God "hath delivered us from the power of darkness, and hath translated us into the kingdom of his dear Son: in whom we have redemption through his blood, even the forgiveness of sins."

The Satanic sowing of the wicked throughout the world, and in particular within the bounds of professing Christendom, is done secretly and surreptitiously even "while men slept" (v. 25). At the outset it may seem difficult to differentiate the unbeliever from the believer, but soon the difference appears. There are those who think they should root out the wicked by forcibly removing the tares, but they were warned by the Saviour not so to do (vv. 28-30).

77

Jesus said with the authority of finality that this age will come to an end. The present condition of the world will not go on forever. During His lifetime He made frequent reference to the judgment of the wicked which will take place at the "great white throne" (Revelation 20:11-15), and also of the judgment of believers at "the judgment seat of Christ" (II Corinthians 5: 10). The Lord spoke of those who build their house upon the sand and not upon a rock (Matthew 7:24-28). At His coming again there will be separation of the unsaved and the saved. He likened the suddenness of that coming time of separation to the flood of Noah's day, saying,

> So shall also the coming of the Son of man be. Then shall two be in the field; the one shall be taken, and the other left. Two women shall be grinding at the mill; the one shall be taken, and the other left. Watch therefore: for ye know not what hour your Lord doth come (Matthew 24:39-42).

It seems to me that as the present age increases in intensity of conflict and commotion, spiritual, political, military, economic, social, racial, ideological, that the differentiation between the tares and the wheat becomes more apparent. There is restlessness everywhere and at every level of life, likened in the Scriptures to the raging of the seas. Luke 21:25-28 declares:

> And there shall be signs in the sun, and in the moon, and in the stars; and upon the earth distress of nations, with perplexity; the sea and the waves roaring; men's hearts failing them for fear, and for looking after those things which are coming on the earth: for the powers of heaven shall be shaken. And then shall they see the Son of man coming in a cloud with power and great glory. And when these things begin to come to pass, then look up, and lift up your heads; for your redemption draweth nigh.

The sea is often symbolically used in the Word to describe mankind, as individuals or as nations. In Isaiah 57:20, 21 we read: "But the wicked are like the troubled sea, when it cannot rest, whose waters cast up mire and dirt. There is no peace, saith my God, to the wicked." Revelation 17:15 adds: "And he saith unto me, The waters which thou sawest, where the whore sitteth, are peoples, and multitudes, and nations, and tongues."

To return to the parable of the harvest, as the end of the gospel era draws to its conclusion the iniquity of the wicked, their contempt for Christ, their hatred of the Most High, grows rapidly. In many places blasphemy against God and brutality to one's fellow men have increased so that one contemporary has cried out, "Has God been insulted hereabouts?" At the same time the true wheat of Bible-believing Christians, those who know and love the Saviour in every place whether in lands of gospel light or those in godless gloom and terror, are continuing to ripen for the ingathering of God's harvest home.

The tares are being gathered together as foretold by the Saviour. When iniquity has reached its climax, "The Son of man shall send forth his angels, and they shall gather out of his kingdom all things that offend, and them which do iniquity; and shall cast them into a furnace of fire: there shall be wailing and gnashing of teeth" (Matthew 13:41, 42).

"But gather the wheat into my barn," the Messiah will say to His angel reapers. "Then shall the righteous shine forth as the sun in the kingdom of their Father. Who hath ears to hear, let him hear" (Matthew 13:43).

O Love That Wilt Not Let Me Go

O Love that wilt not let me go,
  I rest my weary soul in Thee;
I give Thee back the life I owe,
That in Thine ocean depths its flow
  May richer, fuller be.

O Light that followest all my way,
  I yield my flick'ring torch to Thee;
My heart restores its borrow'd ray,
That in Thy sunshine's blaze its day
  May brighter, fairer be.

O Joy that seekest me through pain,
  I cannot close my heart to Thee;
I trace the rainbow through the rain,
And feel the promise is not vain
  That morn shall tearless be.

O Cross that liftest up my head,
  I dare not ask to fly from Thee;
I lay in dust life's glory dead,
And from the ground there blossoms red
  Life that shall endless be.

— GEORGE MATHESON

12

THERE the wicked cease from troubling

Why died I not from the womb? . . . For now should I have lain still and been quiet, I should have slept: then had I been at rest, with kings and counsellors of the earth, which built desolate places for themselves; or with princes that had gold, who filled their houses with silver: or as an hidden untimely birth I had not been; as infants which never saw light. There the wicked cease from troubling; and there the weary be at rest. There the prisoners rest together; they hear not the voice of the oppressor. The small and great are there; and the servant is free from his master. Wherefore is light given to him that is in misery, and life unto the bitter in soul; which long for death, but it cometh not; and dig for it more than for hid treasures; which rejoice exceedingly, and are glad, when they can find the grave? Why is light given to a man whose way is hid, and whom God hath hedged in?   — Job 3:11, 13-23

There the wicked cease from troubling; and *there* the weary be at rest.   — Job 3:17

THE experience of Job and the divine purpose found in his experience are summarized succinctly in the New Testament. James 5:11 states: "Behold, we count them happy which endure. Ye have heard of the patience of Job, and have seen the end of the Lord; that the Lord is very pitiful, and of tender mercy."

God had a purpose in allowing the deep trials and overwhelming sorrows to come to Job, but His servant at the time did not understand that the Most High was causing all things to work together for good for His bewildered child. God knew all the time about the prolonged agony of spirit and body for Job. He had expressed to the adversary His complete confidence in the integrity and faithfulness of Job. The record states twice: "And the Lord said unto Satan, Hast thou considered my servant Job, that there is none like him in the earth, a perfect and an upright man, one that feareth God, and escheweth evil?" (Job 1:8; 2:3). To prove to Satan, and likewise to all of mankind through the ages, that a true child of God can pass unscathed through the fires of affliction, God permitted the enemy to do his worst to Job, short of taking his life.

In his anguish of soul and agony of body, Job could not peer behind the scenes to see that all the while he was being buffeted by the "cruel one," God was also cognizant of what was transpiring. "If we could see beyond today," we say. If we could perceive the spiritual conflicts between light and darkness that may be behind all of our bewilderment and suffering, we should be better able to patiently endure.

In *Pilgrim's Progress*, Bunyan gave a little glimpse of that truth in the illustration by the Interpreter. The latter took the pilgrim, Christian, into a room where a fire was burning against a wall, and a man was pouring water on it to extinguish the flame. To Christian's amazement, however, the fire burned brighter and hotter. Then the Interpreter took him behind the wall where he saw a man pouring in oil, secretly as it were, to replenish the fire. Such, explained the Interpreter, is the work of grace in the heart of a believer. Satan seeks in every way to extinguish it, but all the while the Saviour is secretly pouring into that life the oil of the Holy Spirit.

This was also the experience of Job, for unwittingly in his darkness and distress he was drawing upon the grace of God that was sufficient for him. When admonished by others, even by his own wife, to curse God and die, he could reply: "What? shall we receive good at the hand of God, and shall we not receive evil?" (Job 2:10).

From a human viewpoint, however, there appeared to be

for Job only hopelessness and helplessness, pain and perplexity, misery of frame and misunderstanding by his friends. Only those who have gone through the dark night of the soul can begin to appreciate, even faintly, what must have been the experience of God's servant. One can understand, however, that the believer in a condition such as Job was experiencing would long for cessation of this life and the beginning of the life beyond the grave.

Even in his deepest despair Job did not disbelieve that there is a life beyond death, a new life where sorrows have ceased, wrongs righted, tears dried, pain gone and questions answered. Job lived long centuries before the resurrection of the Lord Jesus Christ, and even before the beginning of the Old Testament written revelation, yet he knew by immediate revelation from God that this life is not all, that there is unending life to come.

Glimpses of that wonderful truth shine out through the gloom of Job's dreadful sickness and sorrow. To his friends he asserted:

> For there is hope of a tree, if it be cut down, that it will sprout again, and that the tender branch thereof will not cease. Though the root thereof wax old in the earth, and the stock thereof die in the ground; yet through the scent of water it will bud, and bring forth boughs like a plant. But man dieth, and wasteth away: yes, man giveth up the ghost, and where is he? As the waters fail from the sea, and the flood decayeth and drieth up: so man lieth down, and riseth not: till the heavens be no more, they shall not awake, nor be raised out of their sleep. O that thou wouldest hide me in the grave, that thou wouldest keep me secret, until thy wrath be past, that thou wouldest appoint me a set time, and remember me! If a man die, shall he live again? all the days of my appointed time will I wait, till my change come. Thou shalt call, and I will answer thee: thou wilt have a desire to the work of thine hands (Job 14:7-15).

Even while he was using the analogy of the tree that is cut down and yet sprouts again Job thought for a moment that perhaps the same was not true of a man; but he quickly recovered his assurance and could say, "Thou shalt call, and I will answer thee."

Again we have his strong confidence in the resurrection and in the life that is to be as he cried out:

83

> Oh that my words were now written! oh that they were printed in a book! That they were graven with an iron pen and lead in the rock for ever. For I know that my redeemer liveth, and that he shall stand at the latter day upon the earth: and though after my skin worms destroy this body, yet in my flesh shall I see God: Whom I shall see for myself, and mine eyes shall behold, and not another; though my reins be consumed within me (Job 19:23-27).

This statement of sublime faith has resounded through the ages to assure God's trusting people that their Redeemer does live, that He shall stand on the earth at the latter day, and that when we see Him we shall be like Him for we shall see Him as He is.

Happy is the heart that in darkness and anguish does not cast aspersion upon God. Although utterly perplexed, Job could say:

> Behold, I go forward, but he is not there; and backward, but I cannot perceive him: On the left hand, where he doth work, but I cannot behold him: He hideth himself on the right hand, that I cannot see him: But he knoweth the way that I take: When he hath tried me, I shall come forth as gold. My foot hath held his steps, his way have I kept, and not declined. Neither have I gone back from the commandment of his lips; I have esteemed the words of his mouth more than my necessary food (Job 23:8-12).

God knows the way that I take! I therefore can have complete confidence in His character and be without fearfulness because of His faithfulness. Like Job, I can with patience draw upon God's grace in the time of trial with assurance that the end will explain it all. Although I see no good whatever in the adversity and anguish, somehow it is working together for my good because I do love the Saviour. Persuaded of God's promises and assured of His presence I can have the confidence that He is planning for me even as He told His servant Jeremiah, saying, "I know the plans that I am planning for you, saith Jehovah, plans of welfare and not of calamity, to give you a future and a hope" (Jeremiah 29:11, Rotherham).

A future, in this life and in the life to come. A hope now and also *there* where wicked cease from troubling, where the weary are at rest.

The Quaker poet, John Greenleaf Whittier, expressed the persuasion of Job in these lines:

Alas for him who never sees
The stars shine through his cypress-trees!
Who, hopeless, lays his dead away,
Nor looks to see the breaking day
Across the mournful marbles play!
Who hath not learned, in hours of faith,
The truth to flesh and sense unknown,
That Life is ever lord of Death,
And love can never lose its own!

Thou Art My Rock

Thou art my Rock, O blessed Redeemer,
  Thou art my Refuge where I may hide;
Thou art my Rock to shelter and bless me;
  Ever in Thee I safely abide.

Thou art my Rock when sin is inviting,
  Thou art my Rock when trial is near;
Thou art my Rock when sorrow is smiting,
  Thou art my Rock; why then should I fear?

Thou art my Rock, temptations defying,
  Thou art my Friend unchanging and sure;
Wholly on Thee my soul is relying,
  Ever to keep me faithful and pure.

Thou art my Rock; when kingdom and nation,
  Ruler and crown, have crumbled to dust;
Thou shalt remain my Rock of salvation,
  Rock everlasting, Thee will I trust.

— MRS. C. E. BRECK

13

THEN thou shalt make thy way prosperous

Now after the death of Moses the servant of the Lord it came to
pass, that the Lord spake unto Joshua the son of Nun, Moses' minister, saying, Moses my servant is dead; now therefore arise, go over
this Jordan, thou, and all this people, unto the land which I do give
to them, even to the children of Israel. Every place that the sole of
your foot shall tread upon, that have I given unto you, as I said unto
Moses. From the wilderness and this Lebanon even unto the great
river, the river Euphrates, all the land of the Hittites, and unto the
great sea toward the going down of the sun, shall be your coast.
There shall not any man be able to stand before thee all the days of
thy life: as I was with Moses, so I will be with thee: I will not fail
thee, nor forsake thee. Be strong and of good courage: for unto this
people shalt thou divide for an inheritance the land, which I sware
unto their fathers to give them. Only be thou strong and very cou-
rageous, that thou mayest observe to do according to all the law,
which Moses my servant commanded thee: turn not from it to the
right hand or to the left, that thou mayest prosper whithersoever thou
goest. This book of the law shall not depart out of thy mouth; but
thou shalt meditate therein day and night, that thou mayest observe
to do according to all that is written therein: for then thou shalt make
thy way prosperous, and then thou shalt have good success. Have not
I commanded thee? Be strong and of a good courage; be not afraid,
neither be thou dismayed: for the Lord thy God is with thee whithersoever thou goest.   — Joshua 1:1-9

> *Then* thou shalt make thy way prosperous, and *then* thou shalt
> have good success.   — Joshua 1:8

GOD takes pleasure in the spiritual, material and physical prosperity of His people. Psalm 35, which relates the deep distress and prolonged persecution of the Psalmist, concludes with the triumphant note, "Let them shout for joy, and be glad, that favour my righteous cause: yea, let them say continually, Let the Lord be magnified, which hath pleasure in the prosperity of his servant. And my tongue shall speak of thy righteousness and of thy praise all the day long." Out of dangers and darkness quite beyond our imagination the prophet Jeremiah could testify, "For the Lord will not cast off for ever: But though he cause grief, yet will he have compassion according to the multitude of his mercies. For he doth not afflict willingly nor grieve the children of men" (Lamentations 3:31-33).

Success is not defined nor determined by material factors alone. While a slave in Potiphar's household, Joseph prospered spiritually with the result that there was an overflow of God's blessing even to those who held him in bondage (Genesis 39:3). When in imminent danger to himself and to his country because of an invading army, King Jehoshaphat exhorted his people, "Believe in the Lord your God, so shall ye be established; believe his prophets, so shall ye prosper" (II Chronicles 20:20); with the result that a great victory was won. Of King Uzziah it is recorded that "as long as he sought the Lord, God made him to prosper . . . but when he was strong, his heart was lifted up to his destruction; for he transgressed against the Lord his God . . ." (II Chronicles 26:5, 16). Regarding King Hezekiah, one of the best monarchs of Judah, the divine account states:

> And thus did Hezekiah throughout all Judah, and wrought that
> which was good and right and truth before the Lord his God. And
> in every work that he began in the service of the house of God, and
> in the law, and in the commandments, to seek his God, he did it
> with all his heart, and prospered (II Chronicles 31:20, 21).

Throughout the Scriptures there is frequent warning against materialism lest such prosperity turn an individual or a nation away from God. When the tribes of Israel came out of Egypt

88

they had long testing in the wilderness, and before they entered the land of promise they had this warning:

> When thou hast eaten and art full, then thou shalt bless the LORD thy God for the good land which he hath given thee. Beware that thou forget not the LORD thy God, in not keeping his commandments, and his judgments, and his statutes, which I command thee this day: Lest when thou hast eaten and art full, and hast built goodly houses, and dwelt therein; and when thy herds and thy flocks multiply, and thy silver and thy gold is multiplied, and all that thou hast is multiplied; then thine heart be lifted up, and thou forget the LORD thy God, which brought thee forth out of the land of Egypt, from the house of bondage; . . . and thou say in thine heart, My power and the might of mine hand hath gotten me this wealth (Deuteronomy 8:10-14, 17).

Psalm 62:10 admonishes us that "if riches increase, set not your heart upon them." Proverbs 1:32 adds that "the prosperity of fools shall destroy them."

A tremendous responsibility was placed upon Joshua. For forty years Moses the man of God had been the leader of Israel. But Moses was dead and by the decree of God the burdens of administration had fallen upon Joshua. By a hitherto untrodden way, beset by dangers and difficulties that must have seemed insurmountable, Joshua was to lead the tribes over the Jordan and conquer the land of Canaan. At the outset the Most High gave Joshua a clear and ringing promise: "Every place that the sole of your foot shall tread upon, that have I given unto you, as I said unto Moses" (Joshua 1:3). Furthermore, there was assurance of God's unfailing presence with His servant, for He assured Joshua that "as I was with Moses, so I will be with thee: I will not fail thee, nor forsake thee" (Joshua 1:5).

The realization of these promises was conditioned on Joshua's firm and unfaltering obedience to the revelation of God given in His Word through Moses. Joshua was not to turn "from it to the right hand nor to the left," nor was it to depart out of his mouth; "but thou shalt meditate therein day and night, that thou mayest observe to do according to all that is written therein." As a result, *then* his way would be prosperous, and *then* he would have good success.

This principle of stating cause and effect, the implicit obedience to the Scriptures with consequent success, was later spelled out in the first Psalm in the description of one who has the blessing of God:

> Blessed is the man that walketh not in the counsel of the ungodly, nor standeth in the way of sinners, nor sitteth in the seat of the scornful. But his delight is in the law of the LORD; and in his law doth he meditate day and night. And he shall be like a tree planted by the rivers of water, that bringeth forth his fruit in his season; his leaf also shall not wither; and whatsoever he doeth shall prosper (vv. 1-3).

To trust God with all of one's heart and to obey all His Word is the secret of a life that is successful and satisfying. Irrespective of outward circumstances there is inward strength and joy in being a hearer of the Word of God and then a faithful doer of its commands. If and when we do our part, *then* God will do His.

14

THEN ye shall return unto the land

And to the Reubenites, and to the Gadites, and to half the tribe of Manasseh, spake Joshua, saying, Remember the word which Moses the servant of the LORD commanded you, saying, The LORD your God hath given you rest, and hath given you this land. Your wives, your little ones, and your cattle, shall remain in the land which Moses gave you on this side Jordan; but ye shall pass before your brethren armed, all the mighty men of valour, and help them; until the LORD have given your brethren rest, as he hath given you, and they also have possessed the land which the LORD your God giveth them: then ye shall return unto the land of your possession, and enjoy it, which Moses the LORD's servant gave you on this side Jordan toward the sunrising.

And they answered Joshua, saying, All that thou commandest us we will do, and whithersoever thou sendest us, we will go. According as we hearkened unto Moses in all things, so will we hearken unto thee: only the LORD thy God be with thee, as he was with Moses. Whosoever he be that doth rebel against thy commandment, and will not hearken unto thy words in all that thou commandest him, he shall be put to death: only be strong and of a good courage.
— Joshua 1:12-18

Then ye shall return unto the land of your possession, and enjoy it . . .   — Joshua 1:15

"AND we won't be back 'til it's over, over there!"

This refrain marked the conclusion of the famous marching song of the First World War entitled "Over There!" We sang it as recruits in training camps in the States and on troop trains destined for ports of embarkation. The band played it over and over as the troopship moved slowly from the dock out into the North River and steamed down to the lower bay of New York Harbor to join the convoy that sailed sometime during the night with destination "somewhere in France." It expressed the determination of the doughboys of that day to fulfill their duty to their country until the task had been concluded by complete victory over our enemies.

"Over there," in substance, was the decision made by the tribes of Reuben, Gad and half the tribe of Manasseh. They had requested of Moses to receive the lands conquered on the east side of the Jordan River, and had secured them on the condition that the soldiers of those tribes would accompany the other nine and one-half tribes over the Jordan until the conquest of the land was completed (see Numbers 32). They had given Moses assurance, ". . . but we ourselves will go ready armed before the children of Israel, until we have brought them unto their place . . . we will not return unto our houses, until the children of Israel have inherited every man his inheritance" (Numbers 32:17, 18). In reply Moses had made them the stipulation, "If ye will do this thing . . . this land shall be your possession before the LORD; but if ye will not, behold, ye have sinned against the LORD: and be sure your sin will find you out" (Numbers 32:20, 22, 23).

Joshua now reminded them to keep their promise and to go in the vanguard of the army as it crossed the Jordan. He could give them no assurance as to how long the men would be in the conflict nor how many of them would be able to return to their families and their lands. His word to them was, "Until the LORD have given your brethren rest, as he hath given you, and they also have possessed the land which the LORD your God giveth them: *then* ye shall return unto the land of your possession, and enjoy it . . . ."

It is our responsibility to complete whatever assignment God may give to us, and *then* we may turn to other prospects and possibilities. It may be that we have promised someone to be of help when needed and sooner or later the request for aid comes to us. Whether or not it is convenient for us to give up what we are doing, to respond wholeheartedly to that request is a matter of our integrity and honor. The Scriptures state clearly: "Withhold not good from them to whom it is due, when it is in the power of thine hand to do it. Say not unto thy neighbour, Go, and come again, and to morrow I will give; when thou hast it by thee" (Proverbs 3:27, 28).

Perhaps we have made a promise to the Lord. Ecclesiastes 5:2, 4 and 5 apply then expressly to us with these instructions: "Be not rash with thy mouth, and let not thine heart be hasty to utter anything before God: for God is in heaven, and thou upon earth: therefore let thy words be few . . . . When thou vowest a vow unto God, defer not to pay it; for he hath no pleasure in fools: pay that which thou hast vowed. Better is it that thou shouldest not vow, than that thou shouldest vow and not pay." This principle was spelled out clearly in Deuteronomy 23:21-23 — "When thou shalt vow a vow unto the LORD thy God, thou shalt not slack to pay it: for the LORD thy God will surely require it of thee; and it would be sin in thee. But if thou shalt forbear to vow, it shall be no sin in thee. That which is gone out of thy lips thou shalt keep and perform; even a freewill-offering, according as thou hast vowed unto the LORD thy God, which thou hast promised with thy mouth."

All this is summarized in the exhortation of Psalm 50:14, 15: "Offer unto God thanksgiving; and pay thy vows unto the most High: And call upon me in the day of trouble: I will deliver thee, and thou shalt glorify me." You may recall that this is the Scripture that Daniel Defoe used as the theme of his immortal book of adventure, *Robinson Crusoe*. Again and again in times of greatest need because of disease or danger, Crusoe's attention was called to the promise of God's deliverance, and through his awareness that God was answering his prayers he learned that his part was to pay the vows which he had made to the Almighty.

After passing through affliction that seemed like going through fire and through water, the Psalmist was brought into a place of peace and prosperity, with the result that he said: "I will go into thy house with burnt offerings: I will pay thee my vows, which my lips have uttered, and my mouth hath spoken, when I was in trouble" (Psalm 66:13, 14). Like him, we are to fulfill all the obligations we have assumed, whether to man or to God. Having put the hand to the plow we are not to turn back nor even look back.

The Corinthian Christians received from the Apostle Paul this counsel regarding their stewardship:

> For ye know the grace of our Lord Jesus Christ, that, though he was rich, yet for your sakes he became poor, that ye through his poverty might be rich. And herein I give my advice: for this is expedient for you, who have begun before, not only to do, but also to be forward [willing] a year ago. Now therefore perform the doing of it; that as there was a readiness to will, so there may be a performance also out of that which ye have. For if there be first a willing mind, it is accepted according to that a man hath, and not according to that he hath not (II Corinthians 8:9-12).

The principle applies to any service as well as to our stewardship of the substance God has entrusted to us.

The men of Manasseh, Reuben and Gad had the right attitude toward the assignment given them by Joshua. In whatever task is assigned to us our hearts should respond as did theirs: "All that thou commandest us we will do, and whithersoever thou sendest us, we will go" (Joshua 1:16).

That is what transpired for the tribes of Israel. The record concludes:

> And the LORD gave unto Israel all the land which he sware to give unto their fathers; and they possessed it, and dwelt therein. And the LORD gave them rest round about, according to all that he sware unto their fathers: and there stood not a man of all their enemies before them; the LORD delivered all their enemies into their hand. There failed not ought of any good thing which the LORD had spoken unto the house of Israel; all came to pass. Then Joshua called the Reubenites, and the Gadites, and the half tribe of Manasseh, and said unto them, Ye have kept all that Moses the servant of the LORD commanded you, and have obeyed my voice in all that I commanded you: Ye have not left your brethren these many days unto this day, but

have kept the charge of the commandment of the LORD your God. And now the LORD your God hath given rest unto your brethren, as he promised them: therefore now return ye, and get you unto your tents, and unto the land of your possession, which Moses the servant of the LORD gave you on the other side Jordan (Joshua 21:43-22:4).

What gladness of heart to faithfully fulfill all that we have promised. *Then* rest is sweet.

Light After Darkness

Light after darkness, gain after loss,
Strength after weakness, crown after cross;
Sweet after bitter, hope after fears,
Home after wand'ring, praise after tears.

Sheaves after sowing, sun after rain,
Sight after myst'ry, peace after pain;
Joy after sorrow, calm after blast,
Rest after weariness, sweet rest at last.

Near after distant, gleam after gloom,
Love after loneliness, life after tomb;
After long agony, rapture of bliss,
Right was the pathway leading to this.

— FRANCES R. HAVERGAL

15

THERE will I be buried

And Naomi said unto her two daughters in law, Go, return each to her mother's house: the LORD deal kindly with you, as ye have dealt with the dead, and with me. The LORD grant you that ye may find rest, each of you in the house of her husband. Then she kissed them; and they lifted up their voice, and wept. And they said unto her, Surely we will return with thee unto thy people . . . And they lifted up their voice, and wept again: and Orpah kissed her mother in law; but Ruth clave unto her. And she said, Behold, thy sister in law is gone back unto her people, and unto her gods: return thou after thy sister in law. And Ruth said, Intreat me not to leave thee, or to return from following after thee: for whither thou goest, I will go; and where thou lodgest, I will lodge: thy people shall be my people, and thy God my God: Where thou diest, will I die, and there will I be buried: the LORD do so to me, and more also, if ought but death part thee and me. When she saw that she was stedfastly minded to go with her, then she left speaking unto her.

So they two went until they came to Bethlehem.

— Ruth 1:8-10, 14-19

Where thou diest, will I die, and *there* will I be buried . . .

— Ruth 1:17

FOR Ruth, *there* was Bethlehem. As yet she had never been there. She had only heard about Bethlehem and the land of Judah. From her homeland in the mountains of Moab she could

99

see on the far western horizon the hill country of Judea, but it lay beyond the Dead Sea and the hot forbidding valley that marked the natural frontier between the two countries. Undoubtedly, she had heard much about Bethlehem from her husband. He had been born and reared in that little village, and only because of prolonged drought there had he been brought by his parents to the land of Moab. His childhood memories of that place were colored with the fancies and illusions that a child can have. Perhaps during their courting days and the brief years of married life, Chilion had talked again and again of Bethlehem, with the thought that someday he would take Ruth to his homeland.

Also, Ruth had heard of Bethlehem from Naomi, her mother-in-law. Mother and daughter-in-law had been increasingly drawn together, and their love had been firmly cemented by the sorrow which they had shared. First Elimelech, Naomi's husband, had died, and the widowed mother was left with her two teen-age sons. In time both of them married, Mahlon to Orpah and Chilion to Ruth. But further sorrow came to those humble homes in Moab for both Mahlon and Chilion died. In their grief, mother and daughters-in-law were bound together in the common lot of hopelessness experienced by widows in a pagan land.

Then it was that Naomi decided to return to Bethlehem. There was no future whatever for her in Moab and, although she could see but little prospect of good in her homeland, at least she would be among her own people. Orpah and Ruth determined to accompany her. After they had gone part of the way, however, Orpah, with tears, returned to her own people. Not so with Ruth. At all odds, at any cost, irrespective of any difficulties known or unknown she would accompany Naomi anywhere she might go.

Ruth knew that there was bad feeling between the people of Judah and those of Moab. Her ancestors had opposed the passage of the Israelites through their land when the latter came out of Egypt. Her head might be saying to her that she had everything to gain by staying in Moab and possibly everything to lose by going into the unknown land of Judea; but her heart

100

said, "Whither thou goest, I will go; and where thou lodgest I will lodge: thy people shall be my people, and thy God my God . . . ."

Such is the expression of true faith in God. Although Ruth did not have understanding of such things, hers was the heart of those who all down the generations have come to recognize themselves as "strangers and pilgrims in the earth," desiring "a better country." By human ties she was attached to Moab, but a far stronger inner impulse impelled her to go onward to Bethlehem. Her choice was made.

Ruth had discerned something in her mother-in-law that had created a desire in her to be with Naomi's people and to know her God. It would seem, on the surface, that Naomi had not been much of a testimony to her daughter-in-law, and the story tells us that she was returning to Bethlehem in bitterness of spirit. But behind and beyond her grief and disillusionment there was something of faith in God, something of resignation to the will of the Most High, something of awareness of God's presence with her. And Ruth had been blessed by her association with Naomi.

Thus it can be with us if, in apparent defeat through utter desolation of heart, we continue to trust God, to walk increasingly with Him and to long for Him because we really do love Him, even though nowhere in our present experience can we find God. Unconsciously we are affecting others, either drawing them toward the Lord or away from Him.

Ruth may or may not have heard from Naomi the story of Isaac and of his bride who came from a distant land. However, the heart attitude of the two young women was much the same. When Abraham's servant arrived in Mesopotamia, after his long journey from Palestine, and found the house of Nahor, he was persuaded that Rebekah was God's choice for Isaac, his master's son. Earnestly he presented the request to Rebekah's family. When they made inquiry of their daughter, "Wilt thou go with this man?" She immediately replied, "I will go" (Genesis 24:58). Rebekah had never been in Palestine but she would go *there* because somehow she perceived in her heart, perhaps dimly, that *there* was the place of God's choosing for her.

101

Ruth's choice had been made. She concluded her decision with words of finality: "Where thou diest, will I die, and there will I be buried: the LORD do so to me, and more also, if ought but death part thee and me." The reward for her decision was far beyond the wildest imagination of Ruth or Naomi, or of anyone in Bethlehem for that matter. Willing to do anything she could to help Naomi she took the place of the poor who gleaned in the fields of grain after the reapers had gone through. Because of her faithfulness to her mother-in-law she came into favor with the people of Bethlehem and with Boaz, the owner of those fields. Because of her humility, Ruth came to honor. It was *there* in those fields that she heard the gracious words of Boaz:

> It hath fully been shewed me, all that thou hast done unto thy mother in law since the death of thine husband: and how thou hast left thy father and thy mother, and the land of thy nativity, and art come unto a people which thou knewest not heretofore. The LORD recompense thy work, and a full reward be given thee of the LORD God of Israel, under whose wings thou art come to trust (Ruth 2: 11, 12).

It was *there* that Ruth was married to Boaz, and thus became an ancestress of the Lord Jesus Christ.

Like a River Glorious

Like a river glorious is God's perfect peace,
Over all victorious in its bright increase;
Perfect, yet it floweth fuller ev'ry day,
Perfect, yet it groweth deeper all the way.

Hidden in the hollow of His blessed hand,
Never foe can follow, never traitor stand;
Not a surge of worry, not a shade of care,
Not a blast of hurry moves the Spirit there.

Ev'ry joy or trial falleth from above,
Traced upon our dial by the Sun of Love.
We may trust Him fully all for us to do:
They who trust Him wholly find Him wholly true.

— FRANCES R. HAVERGAL

16

THERE the Lord commanded

> Behold, how good and how pleasant it is for brethren to dwell to-
> gether in unity! It is like the precious ointment upon the head, that
> ran down upon the beard, even Aaron's beard: that went down to
> the skirts of his garments; as the dew of Hermon, and as the dew
> that descended upon the mountains of Zion: for there the LORD com-
> manded the blessing, even life for evermore.   — Psalm 133

> . . . *there* the LORD commanded the blessing . . . — Psalm 133:3

THE Bible has much to say about the blessing of God. That
blessing is both spiritual and material, both personal and national.
Proverbs 10:22 declares: "The blessing of the LORD, it maketh
rich, and he addeth no sorrow with it."

Material prosperity for Israel of old was promised in Leviticus 26:3-13. This was summarized in Deuteronomy 28:8: "The
LORD shall command the blessing upon thee in thy storehouses,
and in all that thou settest thine hand unto; and he shall bless
thee in the land which the LORD thy God giveth thee."

At the conclusion of the Old Testament came the Word of
the Lord through Malachi:

> Bring ye all the tithes into the storehouse, that there may be meat in
> mine house, and prove me now herewith, saith the LORD of hosts,
> if I will not open you the windows of heaven and pour you out a

blessing, that there shall not be room enough to receive it. And I will rebuke the devourer for your sakes, and he shall not destroy the fruits of your ground; neither shall your vine cast her fruit before the time in the field, saith the LORD of hosts. And all nations shall call you blessed: for ye shall be a delightsome land, saith the LORD of hosts (Malachi 3:10-12).

God does take pleasure in the welfare of His people, both physical and spiritual. The psalmist concluded on that note, as he sang: "Let them shout for joy, and be glad, that favour my righteous cause: yea, let them say continually, Let the LORD be magnified, which hath pleasure in the prosperity of his servant . . . ." (Psalm 35:27). John, the beloved apostle, wrote by the Holy Spirit:

> Beloved, I wish above all things that thou mayest prosper and be in health, even as thy soul prospereth. For I rejoiced greatly, when the brethren came and testified of the truth that is in thee, even as thou walkest in the truth. I have no greater joy than to hear that my children walk in truth (III John 2-4).

All of God's blessings are summarized in Ephesians 1:3: "Blessed be the God and Father of our Lord Jesus Christ, who hath blessed us with all spiritual blessings in heavenly places in Christ."

A basic condition for the blessing of God upon His people is unity of spirit among them. Where hearts are at one, there the Omnipotent Lord can be among His people in power and blessing. Of Gideon and his little band of three hundred stout-hearted men, it is recorded that "they stood every man in his place round about the camp: and all the host [of the enemy] ran, and cried, and fled" (Judges 7:21).

At the dedication of the temple in Solomon's day the divine record declares:

> It came even to pass, as the trumpeters and singers were as one, to make one sound to be heard in praising and thanking the LORD; and when they lifted up their voice with the trumpets and cymbals and instruments of musick, and praised the LORD, saying, For he is good; for his mercy endureth for ever: that then the house was filled with a cloud, even the house of the LORD; so that the priests could not stand to minister by reason of the cloud: for the glory of the LORD had filled the house of God (II Chronicles 5:13, 14).

106

It was on the day of Pentecost when all the disciples "were all with one accord in one place" (Acts 2:1) and after "all continued with one accord in prayer and supplication" (Acts 1:14) that the Holy Spirit came to them. God's presence became apparent among them, both in Old Testament days and in those of the New Testament, when His people were "likeminded, having the same love, being of one accord, of one mind" (Philippians 2:2). Where "brethren dwell together in unity" *there* is the Lord's blessing.

Where there is the Lord's presence among His people, as on the day of Pentecost, there is likewise His power. As a result of the unity of heart among those early disciples and the power of the Holy Spirit, thousands were converted. The account of that first Christian community states that

> They continued stedfastly in the apostles' doctrine and fellowship, and in breaking of bread, and in prayers. And fear came upon every soul: and many wonders and signs were done by the apostles. And all that believed were together, and had all things common; and sold their possessions and goods, and parted them to all men, as every man had need. And they, continuing daily with one accord in the temple, and breaking bread from house to house, did eat their meat with gladness and singleness of heart, praising God, and having favour with all the people. And the Lord added to the church daily such as should be saved (Acts 2:42-47).

That experience has sometimes been confused by being described as "Christian Communism." Communism has become a concept, political and economic in nature, to describe a system of government that is totalitarian, one in which the land and its resources are the property of the state and thus, in theory, all workers are employees of the government. It is likewise authoritarian in that the government has complete control over every area of life with a despotism more deadly and domineering than known to any of the autocracies of old. Twentieth-century communism and Christianity are mutually exclusive concepts. One is wholly atheistic and despotic, while the other operates basically on love for God and for one's fellow men.

That first church in Jerusalem was a small and persecuted assembly of believers which, under the power of the Holy Spirit, gave wonderful witness of the Gospel by word and by life. Under the circumstances that then existed it was most helpful that they had things in common so as to make provision for the many needy ones who lost all their possessions upon becoming Christians. Their experience is not a pattern for all Christians in all ages and under all conditions. However, the basic truth remains that when hearts are at one in the Lord and the Holy Spirit is present in unfettered grace and power that there is this mutual love and devotion one to the other.

When Christians are fully united in spirit, then there can be prevailing prayer. The early believers were under severe pressures and their leaders were threatened that they should not speak in the name of the Lord Jesus Christ. As a result, the Christians assembled together and gave themselves to prayer (Acts 4:23-30). The result of such united and earnest intercession was that "the place was shaken where they were assembled together; and they were all filled with the Holy Ghost, and they spake the word of God with boldness" (Acts 4:31). When the Apostle Peter was imprisoned and condemned to death, "prayer was made without ceasing of the church unto God for him" (Acts 12:5) with the result that he was miraculously delivered from the prison on the night before he was to be beheaded.

"Behold, how good and how pleasant it is for brethren to dwell together in unity!" Such pleasantness results from peace among themselves as well as from the presence of God in their midst and the power of prevailing prayer. In James 3:13-16 we have the exhortation and warning regarding strife among believers. Under such conditions there is no dwelling together in unity, and as a result the blessing of God is lacking. In contrast to this wisdom, described as being earthy, human, devilish, there is its opposite as is further stated in that same portion: "But the wisdom that is from above is first pure, then peaceable, gentle, and easy to be intreated, full of mercy and good fruits, without partiality, and without hypocrisy. And the fruit of righteousness is sown in peace of them that make peace" (James 3:17, 18).

It is the earnest desire of the Saviour that Christians have the same spirit among themselves as that which exists between God the Father and God the Son. He prayed

108

that they all may be one, as thou, Father, art in me, and I in thee, that they also may be one in us: that the world may believe that thou hast sent me. And the glory which thou gavest me I have given them; that they may be one, even as we are one: I in them, and thou in me, that they may be made perfect in one; and that the world may know that thou hast sent me, and hast loved them, as thou hast loved me (John 17:21-23).

That unity is one of spirit and life, not of organization made by man. We can be one in heart and dwell together in unity although we may worship God in separate assemblies and serve Him in different parts of the world.

"*There* the Lord commanded the blessing, even life forevermore!" The fellowship of God's people is the place of His favor. *There* is a state of heart rather than a place or body, something spiritual more than physical.

17

THERE we sat down

By the rivers of Babylon, there we sat down, yea, we wept, when we remembered Zion. We hanged our harps upon the willows in the midst thereof. For there they that carried us away captive required of us a song; and they that wasted us required of us mirth, saying, Sing us one of the songs of Zion. How shall we sing the Lord's song in a strange land? If I forget thee, O Jerusalem, let my right hand forget her cunning. If I do not remember thee, let my tongue cleave to the roof of my mouth; if I prefer not Jerusalem above my chief joy. Remember, O Lord, the children of Edom in the day of Jerusalem; who said, Rase it, rase it, even to the foundation thereof. O daughter of Babylon, who art to be destroyed; happy shall he be, that rewardeth thee as thou hast served us. Happy shall he be, that taketh and dasheth thy little ones against the stones.
— Psalm 137:1-9

By the rivers of Babylon, *there* we sat down . . . *there* they that carried us away captive required of us a song.   — Psalm 137:1, 3

IMPRECATORY Psalms like 137 have always been a perplexity to Bible believers and a point of strong criticism against the Scriptures on the part of unbelievers. Some have sought to justify such Psalms because they alleged to reflect the age in which they were written, a time before the further revelation of the

111

New Testament and of the person of the Lord Jesus were made known. Such explanation, however, hardly seems valid.

The true explanation of such Psalms, in my opinion, is that they constitute the expression of burning anger against diabolic depravity and degradation of those who hate God and are hateful to mankind. Only a high sense of divine righteousness and human justice is capable of great indignation against injustice, indignities and injuries to one's fellow men. Who is not incensed and furious over cruelty to little children? Only a people who had suffered as much as did the Jews during the Second World War could appreciate their attitude and action in regard to Adolph Eichmann, the Nazi mastermind largely responsible for the massacre of more than six-million sons of Abraham. The exiles from satellite countries overrun by communism have justifiable hatred for the inhumanity of callously cruel conquerors.

The remnant of Judah had gone into captivity during the days of the prophet Jeremiah because of their continued perversity and wickedness, their shameful idolatry and their sin. They were in Babylon under the judgment of God who had used the Chaldean armies as His sword. But the conquerors were unnecessarily cruel. At the time of the restoration, when seventy years of captivity were concluded, God taught His people through the prophet Zechariah: "Thus saith the Lord of hosts; I am jealous for Jerusalem and for Zion with a great jealousy. And I am very sore displeased with the heathen [the nations] that are at ease; for I was but a little displeased, and they helped forward the affliction" (Zechariah 1:14, 15). The Most High was expressing His displeasure with His own people, but the affliction applied by their enemies was more than necessary. It was as though a man were to punish a rebellious child with a stick but instead used a great whip and a bar of iron. The captives had no recourse against the injuries and indignities heaped upon them but to call upon God for help. With remorse they remembered their days in Jerusalem and with longing they prayed to be restored.

"*There* we sat down." By the rivers of Babylon. They were *there* because of their disobedience and sinfulness, individual and national. Their fathers and they had been warned earnestly and emphatically by prophets such as Habakkuk and Jeremiah, but to no avail. At long last the judgment of God had to fall upon their land, with the result that they were no longer living under the shadow of Mount Zion but rather were in bondage beside the broad rivers of Babylon. This was not a place of their choosing, but now they had no choice.

"But *there* they that carried us away captive required of us a song," the Israelites wailed. No doubt they questioned, as we sometimes do, was not the judgment of God upon us enough, and should our enemies jeer at us? Should they add sarcasm to our servitude and make our bondage bitter by their coarse jesting about our God? There in Babylon they understood what David meant in Psalm 42:10 when he said, "As with a sword in my bones, mine enemies reproach me; while they say daily unto me, Where is thy God?"

We likewise may be *there* under the judgment of God, because of our own or someone else's disobedience to His revealed will. The cause for divine judgment may be clearly understood by us or only dimly discerned at best. At any rate, the heart has no song because the harp is on the willow tree, and we find ourselves to be hopeless and helpless, friendless, without any future of gladness.

The shadow across our spirit seems to come from the willow trees, whereas actually it may be the shadow of the Almighty. It can be that we have been brought into silence so as to learn to be still and thus know that the Lord is God (Psalm 46:10). It may be that we are under the judgment of God that we may learn His ways and discern His righteousness. While *there* we may learn what the Most High meant in Isaiah 26:7, 8 wherein we read, "The way of the just is uprightness: thou, most upright, dost weigh the path of the just. Yea, in the way of thy judgments, O LORD, have we waited for thee; the desire of our soul is to thy name, and to the remembrance of thee."

Likewise we may learn that the Lord's discipline is designed for our good and is an indication of His love for us. Then we can understand more clearly the exhortation in Hebrews 12:

My son, despise not thou the chastening [discipline] of the Lord, nor faint when thou art rebuked of him: For whom the Lord loveth he

113

chasteneth, and scourgeth every son whom he receiveth. If ye endure chastening, God dealeth with you as with sons; what son is he whom the father chasteneth not? . . . Now no chastening for the present seemeth to be joyous, but grievous: nevertheless afterward it yieldeth the peaceable fruit of righteousness unto them which are exercised thereby (Hebrews 12:5-7, 11).

God had a purpose in allowing His people to be in long captivity in Babylon. When they returned to the land of their fathers they had been completely cured of idolatry.

Can we try to sing when others taunt us about our failures? Can we praise God in our pain and perplexity? Can we bless His name in our bewilderment because of the brutality of our persecutors?

Beneath the conclusion of this 137th Psalm, with its outward appearance of vindictiveness, there is the awareness of the vindication of God. In His time and way He would redeem His repentant people and bring His judgment upon their persecutors. Though God in loving chastisement sometimes puts His people *there*, nevertheless He will maintain the cause of the afflicted and the right of the poor.

18

THEN said I, "Here am I"

In the year that king Uzziah died I saw also the Lord sitting upon a throne, high and lifted up, and his train filled the temple. Above it stood the seraphims: each one had six wings; with twain he covered his face, and with twain he covered his feet, and with twain he did fly. And one cried unto another, and said, Holy, holy, holy, is the LORD of hosts: the whole earth is full of his glory. And the posts of the door moved at the voice of him that cried, and the house was filled with smoke.

Then said I, Woe is me! for I am undone; because I am a man of unclean lips, and I dwell in the midst of a people of unclean lips: for mine eyes have seen the King, the LORD of hosts. Then flew one of the seraphims unto me, having a live coal in his hand, which he had taken with the tongs from off the altar. And he laid it upon my mouth, and said, Lo, this hath touched thy lips; and thine iniquity is taken away, and thy sin purged. Also I heard the voice of the LORD, saying, Whom shall I send, and who will go for us? Then said I, Here am I; send me.   — Isaiah 6:1-8

Then said I, here am I; send me.   — Isaiah 6:8

NOT infrequently one *then* is followed my another in something of a spiritual chain reaction. When the young prophet had the vision of the Lord he then saw his own sinfulness (6:5). Then it was that an angelic being brought cleansing to him (6:6). When Isaiah heard the word of the Lord then he re-

117

sponded, "Here am I; send me." And if that were not enough, upon further instructions from the Most High the prophet responded, "Then said I, Lord, how long?" (6:11).

It would appear that the call of the Almighty, "Whom shall I send, and who will go for us?" was not directed to Isaiah or to anyone in particular. The call of God is something like the call of the sea or the call of the wild. Only the heart that is attuned to that call will hear it. Others, equally intelligent or even more so, can be utterly oblivious to such a call.

It is for that reason that the Scriptures reiterate the need of our receiving the call of God so as to respond to it. To all the churches in the apocalypse there is the exhortation, "He that hath an ear to hear, let him hear" (Revelation 2:7). Of the Israelites it is recorded in Psalm 106:24, 25: "Yea, they despised the pleasant land, they believed not his word: but murmured in their tents, and hearkened not unto the voice of the LORD." Their complaining was so constant that they were unconscious of any call of God.

Again the Psalmist gave the exhortation that we be sensitive to the voice of God saying, "To day if ye will hear his voice, harden not your heart, as in the provocation, and as in the day of temptation in the wilderness: When your fathers tempted me, proved me, and saw my work" (Psalm 95:7-9). Because of hardness of heart they were hard of hearing, and it follows that they therefore did not come to know the ways of God.

This warning is repeated and written with force in Hebrews 3:7-15. We do well to be both hearers and doers of this earnest and searching word:

> Wherefore (as the Holy Ghost saith, To day if ye will hear his voice, harden not your hearts, as in the provocation, in the day of temptation in the wilderness: when your fathers tempted me, proved me, and saw my works forty years. Wherefore I was grieved with that generation, and said, They do alway err in their heart; and they have not known my ways. So I sware in my wrath, They shall not enter into my rest.) Take heed, brethren, lest there be in any of you an evil heart of unbelief, in departing from the living God. But exhort one another daily, while it is called To day; lest any of you be hardened through the deceitfulness of sin. For we are made

partakers of Christ if we hold the beginning of our confidence sted-fast unto the end; while it is said, To day if you will hear his voice, harden not your hearts, as in the provocation.

The hardening of heart is caused by the deceitfulness of sin which in turn inclines the heart through its unbelief to depart from the living God. Contrariwise, we are to be sensitive to sin and repentant so we can have sensitivity of heart to hear the voice of the living God. The Saviour Himself emphasizes that same truth saying, "He that hath ears to hear, let him hear" (Mark 4:9) and again, "Take heed *what* ye hear" (Mark 4:24) and again, "Take heed therefore *how* ye hear" (Luke 8:18). We are to be careful both as to the content of what we hear and the manner in which we listen.

Isaiah's preparation of heart to hear and to obey the call of God is very instructive for us. He did not immediately become aware of the divine summons, "Whom shall I send?" He experienced, rather, a series of steps in preparation.

It was "In the year that king Uzziah died" that the young prophet had his vision of the Almighty. We do not know his heart attitude at the time other than that he quite possibly shared the grief of his people at the death of their monarch and their concern over the inexperience of Jotham, the new king. Isaiah was undoubtedly a man of ability and great promise, and perhaps he knew it. Those were days of controversy and intrigue. Quite possibly Isaiah was quick to speak his persuasion. At any rate, when in a vision he had a glimpse of the Holy One, the immediate reaction was an awareness of his own sinfulness and that of his people.

As long as we walk in the light of human standards of morality we can be respected by others and tempted to become smug and self-satisfied. We are not inclined to make minute differentiation between right and wrong according to the full light of God's Word, but we are content to remain in an area of relatively neutral gray between the white of God's light and the black of sin. However, when once we see the Lord there is no gray, there is only white and black.

We have observed and learned this in seasons of deep heart searching in the presence of God during times of the visitation

119

of God's Holy Spirit. Again and again such has been our experience in Wheaton chapel as the Spirit of the living God has come into our midst, and our response has been to sit with utter contrition of heart and with tears before Him. What we have rationalized as being more right than wrong, more light than dark, turns out to be as black as night under the searchlight of God's Spirit. Then we understand that in such portions as Romans 1:29-31 our own heart is described. We may not do the "wickedness, covetousness, maliciousness" and the like stated in these verses, but the potential is in our hearts by nature, and we need the divine cleansing experienced by Isaiah in his day.

It was when the prophet cried out, "Woe is me! For I am undone; because I am a man of unclean lips" that "*then* flew one of the seraphims unto me, having a live coal in his hand, which he had taken with the tongs from off the altar. And he laid it upon my mouth, and said, Lo, this hath touched thy lips; and thine iniquity is taken away, and thy sin purged" (Isaiah 6:6, 7). Thus in Old Testament times Isaiah experienced the wonderful reality made clear to us in the New Testament when it gives assurance that "If we confess our sins, he is faithful and just to forgive us our sins, and to cleanse us from all unrighteousness" (I John 1:9).

Then it was that Isaiah was in the heart attitude to overhear the call of God and respond to it. The record states: "Then said I, here am I; send me." Now there was willingness for anything that God might say, to go anywhere He might indicate, at anytime He should choose.

An attitude of willingness on our part makes the difference in our activity. The psalmist observed that "Thy people shall be willing in the day of thy power . . ." (110:3). When unwillingness is replaced by eagerness to know and to do the will of God then we surprise ourselves as to what can be accomplished and with what ease. Nothing is difficult or worrisome as long as we are willing. To the eager and responsive Isaiah there came then God's message:

Go, and tell this people, Hear ye indeed, but understand not; and see ye indeed, but perceive not. Make the heart of this people fat,

120

and make their ears heavy, and shut their eyes; lest they see with their eyes, and hear with their ears, and understand with their heart, and convert, and be healed (Isaiah 6:9, 10).

If Isaiah had not been fully prepared in heart and utterly willing for anything God would say to him he might have immediately rebelled against an assignment of this kind. However, his humbled heart had only one response: *"Then* said I, Lord, how long?" To all appearances his ministry was not destined to be a success but, rather, an apparent failure. However, the increasing hopelessness and helplessness made no difference to God's faithful servant who had learned to say, "Here am I; send me."

On our part we are not to be moved by adverse circumstances, by misunderstandings or misrepresentation, by sorrows or losses once we have had a vision of the Sovereign whose grace is sufficient for us. Then our response is anywhere, in any way, for any purpose, for any length of time, for praise or blame. Nothing matters except our being true to the trust committed to us by the high and holy One.

19

THEN Samuel took

And the LORD said unto Samuel, How long wilt thou mourn for Saul, seeing I have rejected him from reigning over Israel? fill thine horn with oil, and go, I will send thee to Jesse the Bethlehemite: for I have provided me a king among his sons. And Samuel said, How can I go? if Saul hear it, he will kill me. And the LORD said, Take an heifer with thee, and say, I am come to sacrifice to the LORD. And call Jesse to the sacrifice, and I will shew thee what thou shalt do: and thou shalt anoint unto me him whom I name unto thee. And Samuel did that which the LORD spake, and came to Bethlehem. And the elders of the town trembled at his coming, and said, Comest thou peaceably? And he said, Peaceably: I am come to sacrifice unto the LORD: sanctify yourselves, and come with me to sacrifice. And he sanctified Jesse and his sons, and called them to the sacrifice.

And it came to pass, when they were come, that he looked on Eliab, and said, Surely the LORD's anointed is before him. But the LORD said unto Samuel, Look not on his countenance, or on the height of his stature; because I have refused him: for the LORD seeth not as man seeth; for man looketh on the outward appearance, but the LORD looketh on the heart. Then Jesse called Abinadab, and made him pass before Samuel. And he said, Neither hath the LORD chosen this. Then Jesse made Shammah to pass by. And he said, Neither hath the LORD chosen this. Again Jesse made seven of his sons to pass before Samuel. And Samuel said unto Jesse, The LORD hath not chosen these. And Samuel said unto Jesse, Are here all thy children? And he said, There remaineth yet the youngest, and, behold, he keepeth the sheep. And Samuel said unto Jesse, Send and fetch him: for we will not sit down till he come hither. And he sent, and brought him in. Now he was ruddy, and withal of a beautiful countenance, and goodly to look to. And the LORD said, Arise, anoint him: for this is he. Then Samuel took the horn of oil, and anointed him in the midst of his brethren: and the Spirit of the LORD came upon David from that day forward. So Samuel rose up, and went to Ramah.   — I Samuel 16:1-13

Then Samuel took the horn of oil, and anointed him in the midst of his brethren: and the Spirit of the LORD came upon David from that day forward.   — I Samuel 16:13

WHEN God measures a man He puts His tape around the heart and not the head.

That truth is firmly written in the Scriptures, although it is not stated in just those words. It was a lesson that Samuel, the judge of Israel, had to learn. It was re-emphasized by the Lord Jesus when He declared, "Judge not according to the appearance, but judge righteous judgment" (John 7:24). One is to learn that face value is not at all necessarily real value, and that although appearance may be appealing it can likewise be deceiving. If Samuel, man of God that he was, needed this lesson (as did the Pharisees in the day of the Lord Jesus), then we also should give close attention to it.

Saul, the first king of Israel, had proved to be a failure; and the Almighty sent His servant Samuel to anoint Saul's successor. Samuel did not know who that person was to be other than that he was one of the sons of Jesse, the Bethlehemite. His instructions included the assurance: "I will show thee what thou shalt do: and thou shalt anoint unto me him whom I name unto thee." Samuel obeyed God's instructions, with the assurance that in His time and way the Most High would make clear who was the man of His choice.

When Jesse called his sons to appear before Samuel it was perfectly natural that the judge of the land would reason that the oldest son would be God's choice. This natural conclusion was re-enforced by the appearance and bearing of Eliab so that Samuel said in his heart, "Surely the LORD's anointed is before him." But Samuel was depending upon outward observation

and human reasoning. Perhaps Samuel had not fully understood the implications of the word from the Lord that he had
spoken to King Saul, saying:

> Thou hast done foolishly: thou hast not kept the commandment
> of the LORD thy God, which he commanded thee: for now would
> the LORD have established thy kingdom upon Israel for ever. But
> now thy kingdom shall not continue: the LORD hath sought him a
> man after his own heart, and the LORD hath commanded him to be
> captain over his people, because thou hast not kept that which the
> LORD commanded thee (I Samuel 13:13, 14).

A man after God's own heart! How was Samuel to evaluate
the heart of Eliab or of the other sons of Jesse? How can any
of us peer beyond outward appearance to know the actuality of
God's evaluation of the heart? If we are sensitive to the leading of God's Spirit we may have some insight in that regard, but
in the last analysis it is God alone who knows the heart. He
knew that Esau would become a "profane man," an irreligious
materialist although a person of commanding appearance and
many talents. His younger brother, Jacob, on the other hand,
had many unfavorable characteristics, but deep within he had a
teachable heart that would love and honor God. Sometimes a
test will show the true quality of the heart. Orpah turned back
to her gods but Ruth held to her mother-in-law Naomi with in-
sistence that she would go anywhere with her. We may make
our estimates and give our personality tests but God alone knows
the heart. Our part is to have our own heart right before Him
and ourselves to be taught by Him to discern the true intent of
the hearts of others.

When Samuel looked favorably upon Jesse's first-born son
he had the inner rebuke from the Lord: "Look not on his countenance, or on the height of his stature; because I have refused
him: for the LORD seeth not as man seeth; for man looketh on
the outward appearance, but the LORD looketh on the heart"
(v. 7). Without doubt Samuel's perplexity increased as one after
another of all seven sons present were disqualified by divine
judgment. Was he somewhat or altogether mistaken as to God's
original guidance that he come to Bethlehem, or had he missed
the indication of divine approval in one of the seven sons? He

therefore inquired, "Are here all thy children?" Thereupon the father said there was one more, the youngest of all, the one therefore who had the most ordinary chore of all, the keeping of the sheep.

The discipline of delay goes deeply into our spirit. It can be that we have begun a project with full assurance that it is the will of God for us only to have the way become increasingly foggy and frustrating so that in bewilderment and disillusionment we are tempted to turn back and give it all up. Nothing seems to work out right and therefore we reason that we must be on the wrong road. This may not be the case at all. Paul and Silas had to keep going onward in a northwesterly direction throughout Asia Minor with no positive guidance as to their destination until they reached the sea coast opposite the great province of Macedonia. Only then did the Word of the Lord come to them with the result that they "endeavored to go into Macedonia, assuredly gathering that the Lord had called" them to preach the gospel there (Acts 16:10). Like Samuel they had to face one divine disapproval of action after another, only to find His plan and purpose in His time.

When David came from the shepherds' fields then the Lord said to Samuel, "Arise, anoint him: for this is he." This is he, the lad who is the man after God's own heart. *Then* there was the divine approval. Then obedience was rewarded and the mission accomplished. Until then Samuel's soul had been deeply exercised by uncertainty and delay; but when God's man came, when God's hour struck, *then* all is made clear.

The test of our faithfulness is to await God's time until *then*. Unquestionably that time is coming!

When All Thy Mercies

When all Thy mercies, O my God,
   My rising soul surveys,
Transported with the view, I'm lost
   In wonder, love, and praise.

Unnumbered comforts on my soul
   Thy tender care bestowed,
Before my infant heart conceived
   From whom these comforts flowed.

When worn with sickness, oft hast Thou
   With health renewed my face;
And when in sins and sorrows sunk,
   Revived my soul with grace.

Ten thousand thousand precious gifts
   My daily thanks employ;
Nor is the least a cheerful heart
   That tastes those gifts with joy.

Through every period of my life
   Thy goodness I'll pursue;
And after death, in distant worlds,
   The glorious theme renew.

Through all eternity to Thee
   A joyful song I'll raise;
But oh, eternity's too short
   To utter all Thy praise!

— JAMES ADDISON

20

THERE did we rejoice

Make a joyful noise unto God, all ye lands: Sing forth the honour of his name: make his praise glorious. Say unto God, How terrible art thou in thy works: through the greatness of thy power shall thine enemies submit themselves unto thee. All the earth shall worship thee, and shall sing unto thee; they shall sing to thy name. Selah. Come and see the works of God: he is terrible in his doing toward the children of men. He turned the sea into dry land: they went through the flood on foot: there did we rejoice in him. He ruleth by his power forever; his eyes behold the nations: let not the rebellious exalt themselves. Selah.   — Psalm 66:1-7

There did we rejoice in him.   — Psalm 66:6

THERE refers to the experience of Israel at the Red Sea. That experience was something to be remembered by succeeding generations. With a strong hand and outstretched arm the Most High brought His people out of the bondage of Egypt and then through the Red Sea. In the generations that followed, whenever the people might be tempted to forget God's power or disbelieve His promises, they were but to remember: "He turned the sea into dry land: they went through the flood on foot!"

The Old Testament experience of the Israelites and their passage through the Red Sea is an excellent illustration of salvation in Christ given to us in the New Testament. In the Scriptures, Egypt is always a type of the world out of which the children of Israel came by way of the Red Sea. Just so is the experience of the penitent sinner who turns from the old life through salvation to walk in newness of life. That experience is graphically described in Ephesians 2:1-8:

> And you hath he quickened, who were dead in trespasses and sins; wherein in time past ye walked according to the course of this world, according to the prince of the power of the air, the spirit that now worketh in the children of disobedience: Among whom also we all had our conversation in times past in the lusts of our flesh, fulfilling the desires of the flesh and of the mind; and were by nature the children of wrath, even as others. But God, who is rich in mercy, for his great love wherewith he loved us, even when we were dead in sins, hath quickened us together with Christ, (by grace ye are saved;) and hath raised us up together, and made us sit together in heavenly places in Christ Jesus: That in the ages to come he might shew the exceeding riches of his grace in his kindness toward us through Christ Jesus. For by grace are ye saved through faith; and that not of yourselves: it is the gift of God.

The Scripture goes on to say that "being justified by faith, we have peace with God through our Lord Jesus Christ" (Romans 5:1), and, "therefore if any man be in Christ, he is a new creature [creation]: old things are passed away; behold, all things are become new" (II Corinthians 5:17). Indeed there is joy and peace and newness of life in believing on Christ.

That joy is the fruit of the Holy Spirit in the life of the new believer (Galatians 5:22, 23), a joy that can be maintained through all the changing circumstances of life. The Christian life is not an easy one, but it can be a succession of triumph in Christ. Many have observed that their real troubles in life did not begin until they received the Lord as Saviour. Then they began to learn that His grace is indeed sufficient for His own, and that the joy of the Lord is their strength.

Directly after calling to mind that *"there* did we rejoice in him," the Psalmist went on to give additional experience in which he found that truth again to prevail. He calls on his people to praise their God for the victorious outcome that came after much adversity: "O bless our God, ye people, and make the voice of his praise to be heard: which holdeth our soul in life, and suffereth not our feet to be moved (Psalm 66:8, 9).

Frequently in the Bible the figure of the silversmith or goldsmith is used. To the Psalmist the season of chastening could be likened to silver being heated in a crucible to the melting point so that the dross can be removed by the silversmith. "Thou hast tried us," he declared, "as silver is tried" (66:10). Of the Lord Jesus there is the prophecy in Malachi 3:2, 3:

> But who may abide the day of his coming? and who shall stand when he appeareth? for he is like a refiner's fire, and like fullers' soap. And he shall sit as a refiner and purifier of silver: and he shall purify the sons of Levi, and purge them as gold and silver, that they may offer unto the LORD an offering in righteousness.

The same figure of speech concerning Israel in the day of the Lord's return is used in Zechariah 13:9:

> And I will bring the third part through the fire, and will refine them as silver is refined, and will try them as gold is tried: they shall call on my name, and I will hear them: I will say, It is my people: and they shall say, The LORD is my God.

In the New Testament there is a similar statement regarding the refining process brought about by persecution, as we read in I Peter 1:7, 8:

> . . . that the trial of your faith, being much more precious than of gold that perisheth, though it be tried with fire, might be found unto praise and honour and glory at the appearing of Jesus Christ: Whom having not seen, ye love; in whom, though now ye see him not, yet believing, ye rejoice with joy unspeakable and full of glory.

In that same Scripture we read:

> Beloved, think it not strange concerning the fiery trial which is to try you, as though some strange thing happened unto you: But rejoice, inasmuch as ye are partaker's of Christ's sufferings; that, when his glory shall be revealed, ye may be glad also with exceeding joy (4:12, 13).

Sometimes one feels caught and helpless — "in a net," as the Psalmist expressed it: "Thou broughtest us into the net: thou layest affliction upon our loins." In the net of adverse circumstances there is no possibility of advance. All activity comes to an end. Life appears wholly useless and pointless; but God is mindful of us there and, indeed, in His loving purposes brings us into that place of silence and forgetfulness on the part of others. God remembered Joseph, though the butler forgot (Genesis 40:23), but until the time that his word came, the word of the Lord tried him.

During his long and unjustified imprisonment, Paul declared repeatedly that he was "the prisoner of the Lord." He was not a prisoner because of the hatred of his enemies or of Roman injustice. He was the prisoner of Jesus Christ who is able to make all things work together for good to anyone who loves Him. Stone walls make no prison and iron chains make no bondage to the soul whom the Saviour has made free. A net laid by our enemies may hinder our feet but cannot handicap the heart.

Affliction has its afterwards, and the day will come when one can say, "It is good for me that I have been afflicted; that I might learn thy statutes" (Psalm 119:71). "For the time being no discipline brings joy but seems grievous and *painful* but afterwards it yields peaceable fruit of righteousness to those who have been trained by it — a harvest of fruit which consists in righteousness . . ." (Hebrews 12:11, *The Amplified New Testament*).

Sometimes there are those who ride roughshod over God's trusting people, "Thou hast caused men to ride over our heads" (Psalm 66:12). Their way may not be right or best for us or even for themselves, but they insist on having their way. Let them have their way. As I look back over life thus far I can see that I have been "kicked upstairs" again and again because someone else was ambitious for a place in which the Lord had placed me. I have learned that as long as one's heart keeps right with the Lord and with others that the Most High is one's unfailing Defender. One learns thereby the meaning of Hebrews 13:5, 6:

> Let your conversation be without covetousness; and be content with such things as ye have: for he hath said, I will never leave thee, nor forsake thee. So that we may boldly say, The Lord is my helper, and I will not fear what man shall do unto me.

"We went through fire and through water," said the Psalmist (66:12). Observe, it was *through* — "but thou broughtest us out into a wealthy place." Literally, it is "a well watered place," an oasis of inexpressible delight in a vast desert. It is the same figure of speech that Jeremiah used of that one whose trust and hope is in the Lord:

> Blessed is the man that trusteth in the LORD, and whose hope the LORD is. For he shall be as a tree planted by the waters, and that spreadeth out her roots by the river, and shall not see when heat cometh, but her leaf shall be green; and shall not be careful in the year of drought, neither shall cease from yielding fruit (17:7, 8).

There did we rejoice in Him. *There* is anywhere under any circumstances in the center of God's will.

Sometimes a Light Surprises

Sometimes a light surprises
  The Christian while he sings;
It is the Lord who rises
  With healing in His wings.
When comforts are declining,
  He grants the soul again
A season of clear shining,
  To cheer it after rain.

In holy contemplation,
  We sweetly then pursue
The theme of God's salvation,
  And find it ever new;
Set free from present sorrow,
  We cheerfully can say —
E'en let th' unknown tomorrow
  Bring with it what it may:

It can bring with it nothing
  But He will bear us through;
Who gives the lilies clothing,
  Will clothe His people too:
Beneath the spreading heavens
  No creature but is fed;
And He, who feeds the ravens,
  Will give His children bread.

Though vine nor fig-tree neither
  Their wonted fruit should bear;
Though all the fields should wither,
  Nor flocks nor herds be there:
Yet God the same abiding,
  His praise shall tune my voice;
For, while in Him confiding,
  I cannot but rejoice.

— WILLIAM COWPER

21

In the mount and be THERE

And the LORD said unto Moses, Come up to me into the mount, and be there: and I will give thee tables of stone, and a law, and commandments which I have written; that thou mayest teach them. And Moses rose up, and his minister Joshua: and Moses went up into the mount of God. And he said unto the elders, Tarry ye here for us, until we come again unto you: and, behold, Aaron and Hur are with you: if any man have any matters to do, let him come unto them. And Moses went up into the mount, and a cloud covered the mount. And the glory of the LORD abode upon mount Sinai, and the cloud covered it six days: and the seventh day he called unto Moses out of the midst of the cloud. And the sight of the glory of the LORD was like devouring fire on the top of the mount in the eyes of the children of Israel. And Moses went into the midst of the cloud, and gat him up into the mount: and Moses was in the mount forty days and forty nights. — Exodus 24:12-18

Come up to me in the mount, and be *there* . . . — Exodus 24:12

GOD'S *there* was the place of revelation for Moses for it was there that he received the Ten Commandments on tablets of stone and the code of laws that were to constitute the basis of God's dealing with His people until the new dispensation at the coming of the Saviour. God has a *there* for you and for me, a time and a place of quiet where we likewise may be still so as

135

to know that He is God and to learn His instructions for us in the light of His revealed Word.

Moses went up into the mountain at God's command. Part of the way he was accompanied by Joshua his servant, but beyond a certain point the man of God went onward alone. He had to leave the people under the jurisdiction of others until his return. In order to meet God on His terms, in His time and at His place, Moses had to be humanly alone. In that solitude he could be silent before the Sovereign of the universe. The quietness would not be disturbed by any outward human interference. His attention could be centered wholly on the revelation to be given to him. Aware of the divine presence, Moses could worship with an awe that is indescribable.

Not every heart knows this humbling and hush before Almighty God, but each one should know that reality for himself. There are occasions when God would call us aside from the routine responsibilities and the many duties that devolve upon our service for Him and for others, thus to have a time alone with Him. In essence He says to some heart, "Come up to me into the mount, and be there." The only response for that heart is that of Moses who obediently went to the place of meeting, though it was in "the midst of the cloud." Even then Moses did not immediately come into God's presence. The cloud covered the mount six days, and "the seventh day he called unto Moses out of the midst of the cloud." Happy is the heart that is obedient to be in the place of God's calling and is willing there to wait for God's presence and promises.

Moses learned to know God far beyond the experience of most believers. God spoke with him as a man speaks with his friend face to face (Deuteronomy 34:10; Exodus 33:11). But on our part we can earnestly desire the maximum of acquaintance-ship with the Lord, much as did the Apostle Paul when he said, "That I may know him!"

The Lord gave us instructions regarding our meeting God *there* and *then*. He said, "But thou, when thou prayest, enter into thy closet, and when thou hast shut thy door, pray to thy Father which is in secret; and thy Father which seeth in secret shall reward thee openly" (Matthew 6:6). There is a wonderful reality about the shut door that enables the heart to enter into God's presence. It may be a material door that must be shut so that the world and all, even one's dear ones and one's responsibilities, are shut outside. Equally so it can be a spiritual door, the door of one's heart, which must be closed to keep out the concerns of the moment so that the heart can commune with God. It was behind the closed door that a widow in Elisha's day found God's provision for her and her sons as she poured olive oil from the tiny container into all the jars, large and small, that had been brought to her (II Kings 4:4).

There is a passage in the writings of the late Dr. A. B. Simpson, founder of the Christian and Missionary Alliance, in which he related the reality of the heart that is quieted and is behind the shut door:

A score of years ago, a friend placed in my hand a book called *True Peace*. It was an old medieval message, and it had but one thought — that God was waiting in the depths of my being to talk to me if I would only get still enough to hear His voice.

I thought this would be a very easy matter, and so began to get still. But I had no sooner commenced than a perfect pandemonium of voices reached my ears, a thousand clamoring notes from without and within, until I could hear nothing but their noise and din.

Some were my own voices, my own questions, some my very prayers. Others were suggestions of the tempter and the voices from the world's turmoil.

In every direction I was pulled and pushed and greeted with noisy acclamations and unspeakable unrest. It seemed necessary for me to listen to some of them and to answer some of them; but God said, "Be still, and know that I am God." Then came the conflict of thoughts for tomorrow, and its duties and cares; but God said, "Be still."

And as I listened, and slowly learned to obey, and shut my ears to every sound, I found after a while that when the other voices ceased, or I ceased to hear them, there was a still small voice in the depths of my being that began to speak with an inexpressible tenderness, power and comfort.

As I listened, it became to me the voice of prayer, the voice of wisdom, the voice of duty, and I did not need to think so hard, or pray so hard, or trust so hard; but that "still small voice" of the Holy Spirit in my heart was God's prayer in my secret soul, was God's answer to all my questions, was God's life and strength for soul and body, and became the substance of all knowledge, and all prayer and all blessing: for it was the living God Himself as my life, my all.

It is thus that our spirit drinks in the life of our risen Lord, and we go forth to life's conflicts and duties like a flower that has drunk in, through the shades of night, the cool and crystal drops of dew. But as dew never falls on a stormy night, so the dews of His grace never come to the restless soul.

God's *there* may mean physically some place of retirement where there can be no interruption. It can be also in the midst of life's multitude of duties, in a busy kitchen or office, that one may have the inner hush of heart and worship in the presence of God.

The late Dr. J. Wilbur Chapman, the American evangelist greatly used of God at home and abroad, related an experience of what it means to be *there* in the presence of God. With Charles N. Alexander as song leader, he was holding services in England. At that time John Hyde, a missionary from India who had become known as "Praying Hyde" because of his ministry of intercession, was en route home to America. The missionary went to the services held by his fellow American. Dr. Chapman wrote:

> At one of our missions in England the audience was extremely small, results seemed impossible but I received a note saying that an American missionary was coming to the town and was going to pray God's blessing upon our work. He was known as "Praying Hyde."
>
> Almost instantly the tide turned. The hall was packed, and my first invitation meant fifty men for Jesus Christ As we were leaving I said, "Mr. Hyde, I want you to pray for me." He came to my room, turned the key in the door, dropped on his knees, waited five minutes without a single syllable coming from his lips. I could hear my own heart thumping and beating. I felt the hot tears running down my face. I knew I was with God. Then with upturned face, down which the tears were streaming, he said: "Oh, God!"
>
> Then for five minutes at least, he was still again, and then when he knew he was talking with God his arm went around my shoulder and there came up from the depth of his heart such petitions for men as I had never heard before. I rose from my knees to know what real prayer was. . . .

After Moses came down from God's *there* he had God's revelation in his hand and head as well as in his heart. Unknown to him, God's glow was in his face, as well as God's glory in his heart. Out of acquaintanceship with the Most High there was for him utter abandonment to the Almighty. Moses, whose heart had begun to burn for God at the burning bush, had become the man of God on the burning mountain of God's *there*. It is our responsibility and opportunity in our day and generation also to know what it means to be in God's *there*.

22

THEN I knew

And Jeremiah said, The word of the LORD came unto me, saying, Behold, Hanameel the son of Shallum thine uncle shall come unto thee, saying, Buy thee my field that is in Anathoth: for the right of redemption is thine to buy it. So Hanameel mine uncle's son came to me in the court of the prison according to the word of the LORD, and said unto me, Buy my field, I pray thee, that is in Anathoth, which is in the country of Benjamin: for the right of inheritance is thine, and the redemption is thine; buy it for thyself. *Then I knew* that this was the word of the LORD. And I bought the field of Hanameel my uncle's son, that was in Anathoth, and weighed him the money, even seventeen shekels of silver. And I subscribed the evidence, and sealed it, and took witnesses, and weighed him the money in the balances.

And I charged Baruch before them, saying, Thus saith the LORD of hosts, the God of Israel; Take these evidences, this evidence of the purchase, both which is sealed, and this evidence which is open; and put them in an earthen vessel, that they may continue many days. For thus saith the LORD of hosts, the God of Israel; Houses and fields and vineyards shall be possessed again in this land.

— Jeremiah 32:6-10; 13-15

Then I knew that this was the word of the LORD. — Jeremiah 32:8

SOMETIMES God's guidance in one's life appears at the outset to be mere fancy, a passing thought, something fortuitous

141

and far fetched with no basis in fact. It seems to you or to me as mere chance, a wandering thought, or even imagination run riot.

The word of the Lord must have appeared that way to His servant, Jeremiah, when God instructed him to buy property in Anathoth. Jeremiah himself was a prisoner "shut up in the court of the prison, which was in the king of Judah's house" (32: 2). The Chaldean army had been besieging Jerusalem for more than a year, and its fall was imminent. In fact, Jeremiah had been imprisoned by King Zedekiah because he had said plainly, "Thus saith the Lord, Behold, I will give the city into the hand of the king of Babylon, and he shall take it" (32:28). The prophet knew, furthermore, that even though his own life would be spared in the fall of Jerusalem, his people would be in captivity in Babylon for seventy years. His uncle's property in Anathoth, Jeremiah's home town, could have no possible value to Jeremiah. Furthermore, it is almost certain at the very time that this word came from God to His servant, Anathoth was in the hands of the enemy. It lies to the north of Jerusalem from which direction the Chaldean forces had come. From every possible viewpoint, humanly speaking, any thought of Jeremiah's purchasing real estate in Anathoth was the greatest folly. A poorer investment could not be imagined.

Nevertheless, God's word was plain to the prophet that a relative, Hanameel, would come to request that the property be purchased. For Jeremiah there was no other course of action than to trust God and obey Him. He was not to precipitate the situation by any inquiry on his own part; his instructions were to buy the field and wait God's time. When, therefore, Hanameel came with the request, "Buy my field, I pray thee, that is in Anathoth, which is in the country of Benjamin . . . buy it for thyself," *then* Jeremiah knew that he had God's clear guidance.

There is a wonderful reality in this matter of assurance regarding the will of God. There is the reality of the immediacy of God the Holy Spirit in speaking to one's heart through the Scriptures or apart from them, so that the will of God is made plain and pertinent to the child of God. What is thus revealed must be obeyed or disobeyed. Quite possibly the revelation has to do with something in the future, and the obedient heart, like Jeremiah, is to be entirely silent until the Word of the Lord is fulfilled.

Let me illustrate. One January night in 1936 I was awakened out of a deep and dreamless sleep into a fully conscious awareness of the Holy Spirit's presence. At that time I was a new instructor at Nyack Missionary College, having entered the faculty in September of the previous year. I was very happy in the teaching of the young people on that lovely hillside overlooking the broad Hudson River. Mrs. Edman and I and the four little boys were as happy as any family could be in that "mount of prayer and blessing." For my part I had no other thought than to continue there at Nyack preparing young people for service at home and abroad.

Then, wholly without any thought or desire on my part, there came in the stillness of the night the inquiry of the Holy Spirit, "What are you going to do about a call to Wheaton?" Wheaton! I had never given Wheaton a thought. I had no desire to leave Nyack, and likewise had no acquaintanceship with Wheaton.

My response may seem ludicrous to you. The inquiry was made twice and at the second time I replied inaudibly (for none of this interview was with outer voice or sound), "Dear Lord, I do not know what I should do about a call to Wheaton. I am disheartened by those who say they have a call to this place or that place but have turned down such invitations, it seems with a tone of smug self-satisfaction. If it is not Thy will that I should go to Wheaton, be pleased that no call should come to me." Thereupon I fell asleep again. The whole matter had been completely committed to the faithful Holy Spirit, so completely that on the morrow I had forgotten all about it. No mention was made of it to anyone.

Some weeks later I saw on a bulletin board a notice of a young people's rally to be held on Long Island with Dr. J. Oliver Buswell Jr., president of Wheaton College, as the speaker. It occurred to me that Mrs. Edman and I might want to go to that rally; but on second thought, as I remembered what the Lord had said to me on that January night, I decided not to go. There

143

could be the possibility that someone at the rally would know both President Buswell and myself and seek to introduce me to him. As far as I understood the will of God, I was to do nothing whatever regarding any possible call to Wheaton College.

Then on the first Saturday of March that year came an invitation from President Buswell to join the Wheaton Faculty. Like Hezekiah of old we spread the letter out before the Lord in prayer. Then I shared with Mrs. Edman in detail the Lord's word to me and my understanding with Him that no call should come if it were not His will.

We both felt that one further bit of cross checking should be done lest in any way we mistake God's guidance. That same Saturday I wrote to two dear friends, faithful prayer warriors who knew the Lord. In a few days from a good Christian brother in Worcester, Massachusetts, came the response, "The Lord says, Go with joy!" The second reply came from California: "Your fleece is wet!"

Thus it was with Jeremiah. When what the Word told him was fulfilled, he "knew that this was the word of the Lord."

Then implies hearing, believing, waiting and finally obeying.

'Tis There!

Oppress'd by noonday's scorching heat,
   To yonder Cross I flee,
Beneath its shelter take my seat —
   No shade like this to me!

Beneath that Cross clear waters burst,
   A fountain sparkling free,
And there I quench my desert thirst —
   No spring like this to me!

For burdened ones, a resting place
   Beside that Cross I see;
Here I cast off my weariness —
   No rest like this for me!

A stranger here, I pitch my tent
   Beneath this spreading tree;
Here shall my pilgrim life be spent —
   No home like this for me!

— HORATIUS BONAR

23

THEN David came to Mahanaim

Then David came to Mahanaim. And Absalom passed over Jordan, he and all the men of Israel with him. . . . And it came to pass, when David was come to Mahanaim, that Shobi the son of Nahash of Rabbah of the children of Ammon, and Machir the son of Ammiel of Lo-debar, and Barzillai the Gileadite of Rogelim, brought beds, and basons, and earthen vessels, and wheat, and barley, and flour, and parched corn, and beans, and lentiles, and parched pulse, and honey, and butter, and sheep, and cheese of kine, for David, and for the people that were with him, to eat: for they said, The people is hungry, and weary, and thirsty, in the wilderness.

— II Samuel 17:24, 27-29

Then David came to Mahanaim. — II Samuel 17:24

WHEN David fled from Jerusalem because of the rebellion led by his son Absalom, he came to Mahanaim on the east side of the Jordan river. There Barzillai came to meet him.

Barzillai is one of my favorite Bible characters. Not much is recorded about him in the sacred Scriptures, but all that we have is of great delight to me. I have always wished that Alexander Whyte, the great Scottish divine of the early part of this century, had included Barzillai in his series of Sunday evening messages on Bible characters.

147

Of Barzillai the Bible states simply that he "was a very aged man, even fourscore years old: and he had provided the king of sustenance while he lay at Mahanaim; for he was a very great man" (II Samuel 19:32).

King David said to Barzillai (II Samuel 19:33-40):

Come thou over with me, and I will feed thee with me in Jerusalem. And Barzillai said unto the king, How long have I to live, that I should go up with the king unto Jerusalem? I am this day fourscore years old: and can I discern between good and evil? can thy servant taste what I eat or what I drink? can I hear any more the voice of singing men and singing women? wherefore then should thy servant be yet a burden unto my lord the king? Thy servant will go a little way over Jordan with the king: and why should the king recompense it me with such a reward? Let thy servant, I pray thee, turn back again, that I may die in mine own city, and be buried by the grave of my father and of my mother. But behold thy servant Chimham; let him go over with my lord the king; and do to him what shall seem good unto thee. And the king answered, Chimham shall go over with me, and I will do him that which shall seem good unto thee: and whatsoever thou shalt require of me, that will I do for thee. And all the people went over Jordan. And when the king was come over, the king kissed Barzillai, and blessed him; and he returned unto his own place. Then the king went on to Gilgal, and Chimham went on with him: and all the people of Judah conducted the king, and also half the people of Israel.

Undoubtedly Barzillai was a wealthy man by the standards of that day with large possessions in land and with flocks of sheep and herds of cattle and camels. His family had lived on the east side of the Jordan ever since the conquest of the land in the days of Joshua when the territory was assigned to the tribes of Reuben, Gad and half of Manasseh. There is no indication that he was in any way related to David. His coming to Mahanaim was entirely an action decided upon because of his affection and confidence in his monarch.

Barzillai was no fair weather friend. He would be loyal to his king irrespective of any danger to himself or to his possessions. At the time of his decision to align himself with the king, Barzillai was most certainly in the minority. The multitudes had gone after Absalom. Many of the king's counselors and captains in his army had gone over to the rebellion, and the forces that fled with the king were much smaller than those of the rebels. From every appearance the rebellion was already a complete success because the capital city and all the territory west of the Jordan with its nine and one-half tribes was already under Absalom's control.

Barzillai's loyalty to David might possibly have meant the loss of his own life; or if he had succeeded in escaping with some of his family and servants his property certainly would have been confiscated. If Barzillai were of the stripe whose principal color is yellow, he would have aligned himself with the armies of Absalom and consequently would have refused to give any aid or comfort whatever to the elderly king and his exhausted troops.

But Barzillai was the kind of friend that sticks closer than a brother. With him patriotism was a matter of profound persuasion, not something that could change like the weather. Loyalty to his king and friend meant more to him than the possible loss of everything he had. He would be openly and unashamedly on David's side, and not some secret sympathizer standing off at great distance to see how the die would be cast. He would stand up and be counted on David's side right then and there. He anticipated the needs of the king and his army for with his friends Shobi and Machir he

brought beds, and basons, and earthen vessels, and wheat, and barley, and flour, and parched corn, and beans, and lentiles, and parched pulse, and honey, and butter, and sheep, and cheese of kine, for David, and for the people that were with him, to eat: for they said, The people is hungry, and weary, and thirsty, in the wilderness (II Samuel 17:28, 29).

Possibly all this was done because of Barzillai's leadership and example. At any rate, the other two friends are not mentioned further in the story. It often happens that when one friend will arise on behalf of someone under pressure, persecution, misrepresentation or malice, so that all seems to be lost, then other friends who might be inclined to be more timid also take courage to stand.

A friend in need is a friend indeed! Happy is the heart that has such a friend and finds that friendship to be strong, sweet, unswerving, undismayed. Something like that was the experience of the Apostle Paul. At a time of perplexity and great difficulty he learned what the coming of a friend can mean. This is his word:

> For, when we were come into Macedonia, our flesh had no rest, but we were troubled on every side; without were fightings, within were fears. Nevertheless God, that comforteth those that are cast down, comforted us by the coming of Titus. And not by his coming only, but by the consolation wherewith he was comforted in you, when he told us your earnest desire, your mourning, your fervent mind toward me; so that I rejoiced the more (II Corinthians 7:5-7).

All of that Barzillai meant to David at Mahanaim.

In Psalm 3, which very possibly was composed at Mahanaim, we get much insight into the feelings of David. It has the title: "A Psalm of David, when he fled from Absalom his son." These are the words of the king in the first part of that Psalm:

> Lord, how are they increased that trouble me! many are they that rise up against me. Many there be which say of my soul, There is no help for him in God. Selah. But thou, O Lord, art a shield for me; my glory, and the lifter up of mine head. I cried unto the Lord with my voice, and he heard me out of his holy hill. Selah. I laid me down and slept; I awaked; for the Lord sustained me. I will not be afraid of ten thousands of people, that have set themselves against me round about (vv. 1-6).

The Lord was indeed David's light and salvation, a lifter up of his head. The Most High used His servant Barzillai to provide the necessary food and shelter for the king and his men when they were hungry, weary and thirsty in the wilderness. Then David could rest because God had heard his prayer for protection and God's servant had brought sustenance for his provision.

The next morning everything looked different to David. Rested in body, refreshed and strengthened with food, and reassured of God's presence with him, he could then be unafraid of the tens of thousands of troops Absalom was leading against him.

In the battle that followed, the rebel son lost his life and his army was scattered. The king was then free to return to his capital city and to resume his sovereignty over his people. In his affection for his friend Barzillai and in appreciation for all he had done for him in risking his life and his fortune, David urged him to live in the royal palace. However, the man of Gilead, then 80 years of age, preferred to remain at home, saying, "Wherefore then should thy servant be yet a burden unto my lord the king?" (19:35). The success of his sovereign and his welfare were all the reward Barzillai would want.

Perhaps the love and loyalty of Barzillai lies behind the observation made by David's son, Solomon: "A friend loveth at all times, and a brother is born for adversity" (Proverbs 17:17).

24

THERE were they in great fear

The fool hath said in his heart, There is no God. Corrupt are they, and have done abominable iniquity: there is none that doeth good. God looked down from heaven upon the children of men, to see if there were any that did understand, that did seek God. Every one of them is gone back: they are altogether become filthy; there is none that doeth good, no, not one. Have the workers of iniquity no knowledge? who eat up my people as they eat bread: they have not called upon God. There were they in great fear, where no fear was: for God hath scattered the bones of him that encampeth against thee: thou hast put them to shame, because God hath despised them. Oh that the salvation of Israel were come out of Zion! When God bringeth back the captivity of his people, Jacob shall rejoice and Israel shall be glad.   — Psalm 53

There were they in great fear, where no fear was . . . —Psalm 53:5

FEAR is not of God.

The Word says plainly that "God hath not given us the spirit of fear, but of power, and of love, and of a sound mind" (II Timothy 1:7). The Amplified Version gives this translation: "For God did not give us a spirit of timidity — of cowardice, of craven and cringing and fawning fear — but [He has given us a spirit] of power and of love and of calm and well-balanced mind *and* discipline *and* self control."

The familiar words of Proverbs 28:1 are a commentary on those who were in great fear, for it states that "The wicked flee when no man pursueth: but the righteous are bold as a lion." God predicted that kind of fear to the unbelieving, disobedient and rebellious saying, "And upon them that are left alive of you I will send a faintness into their hearts in the lands of their enemies; and the sound of a shaken leaf shall chase them; and they shall flee, as fleeing from a sword; and they shall fall when none pursueth" (Leviticus 26:36).

The believer in Christ has access to freedom from fear. The Psalmist testified: "I sought the Lord, and He heard me, and delivered me from all my fears" (Psalm 34:4). In another place he declared: "What time I am afraid, I will trust in thee" (Psalm 56:3). Deliverance from fear seems to depend on two simple factors: first, to look steadily and fearlessly at the fear itself so as to know whether it is imaginary or real, and then to look steadily and confidently to the Strong One who says to us, "Fear thou not, for I am with thee; be not dismayed, for I am thy god" (Isaiah 41:10).

Some illustrations may help us grasp these essential truths. Years ago a young missionary wife confided to us a fear that was overpowering to her. She was afraid of snakes. She was a dedicated missionary and a devoted wife, and when her husband was called to pioneer work in the Amazon jungles she, of course, accompanied him there, but with a fear that did not leave her day nor night. Shortly after her arrival at the place chosen for the new mission station, the fear came to a climax. At that moment she was in a little bamboo shack that was covered with palm leaves to protect her from the rain. Her husband and some friendly Indians were clearing the brush. He called to her to come out to see what had happened. Instinctively she knew what had transpired and from the depths of her heart she said, "Lord, I cannot go out there to see it!" Again her husband called and she arose with the resolve, "Lord, in thy strength I will go." Sure enough, the men had killed a large snake and had tied it by its tail to the limb of a tree. The young missionary walked right up to it, carefully observed its length, girth, colorings and the head nearly severed from the body by the stroke of the machete. "Right there," she testified later, "the Lord took all fear of snakes out of my heart."

A fear can be wholly imaginary, and when faced squarely it vanishes into thin air. A business acquaintance in Wheaton gave me a good illustration of that possibility. During the bank crisis of February, 1933, he was a teller in a local bank. The institution was perfectly solvent but, since many banks over the country were failing, the depositors began to withdraw their funds. Each day he was busy paying some depositors in full. One afternoon he took a moment to look at the length of the line of those waiting when to his dismay Charlie, the laundry man, took his place at the end of the line. The teller knew that Charlie was the largest depositor in the bank and if he should demand payment in full that afternoon there was not ready cash enough to pay him off. The money would be available in the morning, but not that afternoon.

The teller's apprehension increased as the line moved slowly onward. It took nearly an hour before Charlie was the next one to appear at the window. There was nothing to do but to face the worst. Should Charlie ask for his money and be told he could not be paid right now, there would be a panic.

Quietly the Chinese laundry man said, "Can I ask you for something?" "Surely, Charlie," replied the teller, "come around the side of the cage." There was hope that possibly the withdrawal might be postponed until tomorrow. "Can I have a calendar?" was Charlie's astonishing inquiry! He had not come for his money, but for a calendar! My friend still does not know if Charlie really came for his money or just to look over the situation. At any rate, there was a fear which proved to be imaginary.

On the other hand, there are fears that are well-founded. Several years ago I was blinded by retina detachments, first in the right eye and then in the left. After each round of eye surgery, followed by weeks of darkness and pain, I was brought home from the hospital for the continuation of the discipline of darkness.

Then the retina in the left eye broke again. I was aware of what was transpiring, but at first I said nothing to Mrs. Edman. That evening, however, I shared the knowledge with her, and there were tears and prayers on her part for me.

Early the following morning she brought me some toast and coffee, and put on the record player some Bible records that Billy Graham had sent me. In the darkness I listened to several chapters of Isaiah. Thereafter I arose to walk a little for exercise. I had learned how many steps to take in one direction and how to return to the chair where I had been sitting by the record player. I walked back and forth several times, and in my meditation and prayer I wondered if I should ever see again. I stopped in my walking and sought to orient myself toward the campus. I wondered if ever again I would see that lane of maple trees leading up to Blanchard Hall with its tall tower, to be in the office with all of its duties and delights, to be with the students in chapel or to sit on a bench at a football game to see the Orange and Blue triumph over some rival college. Then I turned, only to find that I had lost my sense of direction. I had lost my way and did not know which way to move for fear of stumbling over some unseen object.

Just then, in my helplessness, there came the most wonderful sense of the Lord's presence with assurance that He would never leave me nor forsake me. For some moments I was quiet before Him in worship and gratitude; then moving slowly to the left I found a chair. After that I knew where I was and could direct my steps back to the place from which I had come.

There was a fear that was real. The retina had broken again and that was confirmed by the ophthalmologist later that same morning. There had to be more surgery, more pain, more prolonged darkness, more uncertainty as to any remaining vision when healing would be completed.

But afraid? Who could be afraid when the Lord of Glory is at our side? Of God's children it is said, "He shall not be afraid of evil tidings: his heart is fixed [established], trusting in the LORD" (Psalm 112:7).

There those who know not the Lord can be in great fear. Right *there* those who know Him can be full of faith and therefore fearless.

Take Thou My Hand

Take Thou my hand, and lead me —
  Choose Thou my way!
"Not as I will," O Father,
  Teach me to say.
What though the storms may gather,
  Thou knowest best;
Safe in Thy holy keeping,
  There would I rest.

Take Thou my hand, and lead me —
  Lord, I am Thine!
Fill with Thy Holy Spirit
  This heart of mine:
Then in the hour of trial
  Strong shall I be —
Ready to do, or suffer,
  Dear Lord, for Thee.

Take Thou my hand, and lead me,
  Lord, as I go;
Into Thy perfect image
  Help me to grow.
Still in Thine own pavilion
  Shelter Thou me;
Keep me, O Father, keep me
  Close, close to Thee!

           — JULIA STERLING

25

And THERE rememberest

Ye have heard that it was said by them of old time, Thou shalt
not kill; and whosoever shall kill shall be in danger of the judgment:
but I say unto you, That whosoever is angry with his brother without a cause shall be in danger of the judgment: and whosoever shall
say to his brother, Raca, shall be in danger of the council: but whosoever shall say, Thou fool, shall be in danger of hell fire. Therefore
if thou bring thy gift to the altar, *and there rememberest* that thy
brother hath ought against thee; leave there thy gift before the altar,
and go thy way; first be reconciled to thy brother, and then come and
offer thy gift. Agree with thine adversary quickly, whiles thou art
in the way with him; lest at any time the adversary deliver thee to
the judge, and the judge deliver thee to the officer, and thou be cast
into prison.   — Matthew 5:21-25

Therefore if thou bring thy gift to the altar, and *there* rememberest that thy brother hath ought against thee . . . — Matthew 5:23

FELLOWSHIP with God is impossible if we are out of fellowship with a fellow believer. The Scriptures on this point are very
searching. They say plainly that "If we say that we have fellowship with him [God], and walk in darkness, we lie, and do not
the truth" (I John 1:6). It is perfectly possible to allege that
we are rightly related to the Lord and walking before Him in

uprightness when all the time we are in reality walking in spiritual darkness.

The Bible becomes explicit in this matter of walking in the light or in the darkness. In I John 2:9-11 we read:

> He that saith he is in the light, and hateth his brother, is in darkness even until now. He that loveth his brother abideth in the light, and there is none occasion of stumbling in him. But he that hateth his brother is in darkness, and walketh in darkness, and knoweth not whither he goeth, because that darkness hath blinded his eyes.

Here again we have the allegation that one is walking in the light when in reality he is in darkness so deep that spiritual sight is clouded completely. To detest or to despise a brother in Christ is to be in darkness, irrespective of one's works or deeds.

I recall an evening service in Wheaton Chapel when there came a wonderful sense of God's presence in our midst. As a result, the planned service was set aside that we might wait before the Lord, to pray, to have one's heart searched out before the Lord and to be right with Him. We sat quietly in His presence and I was conscious only of the soft sobbing of broken hearts and occasionally a quiet prayer. Not until I sensed that the service was over did I speak to anyone. Then I walked over to a senior student who had sat with head bowed the entire time.

Sitting down alongside her I inquired, "Bonnie, how goes it?"

"Prexy," she replied without looking up, "it is darkness."

"Why is it darkness?"

In response she pointed to I John 2:9 in the open Bible that she was holding. "Bonnie, do you hate somebody?" I asked. The answer was a nod of her head. "In that case, lassie," I said, "you will never come into the light until that hatred is taken out of your heart."

Then she earnestly prayed for forgiveness and for the courage to do what was right. When she concluded her prayer I added a word of petition and also of praise to the Lord. Then looking up at me through her tears she asked, "Prexy, should I go to see her right now?"

I glanced at the chapel clock and said, "If it is someone close at hand, and you need not tell me who it is, I think it best that you see her first thing in the morning. It is now past eleven o'clock and it would be thoughtful of you not to disturb someone who may have retired. However, go to that person the first thing in the morning. Ask forgiveness for whatever wrong is on your part. Make no reference to any wrong, real or imaginery, that the other person has done. Then come to see me."

The next morning when Bonnie came into the office I did not have to ask her if she had obeyed the Lord. I could see in the light on her face that there was joy in her heart because she was walking again in the light.

Our fellowship one with another is the divine measure of our fellowship with God. The Scripture adds still a further word in I John 3:14-16:

> We know that we have passed from death unto life, because we love the brethren. He that loveth not his brother abideth in death. Whosoever hateth his brother is a murderer: and ye know that no murderer hath eternal life abiding in him. Hereby perceive we the love of God, because he laid down his life for us: and we ought to lay down our lives for the brethren.

We do not pass from death unto life because we love one another, but our assurance of that reality is dependent upon our relationship one with another. Such love is to be a reality, a vital factor in our life, as the Word goes on to say: "My little children, let us not love in word, neither in tongue; but in deed and in truth" (I John 3:18).

In the Sermon on the Mount the Saviour was taking His hearers into the *spirit* of the law, entirely beyond its letter. There is always the human tendency to stress the overt acts of wickedness as being sin, and neglecting the attitude, which in reality is equally sinful. Our Lord was teaching them, and ourselves as well, that the sinfulness of murder is not only in the taking of life but that the hatred which is its root is equally hateful to the Almighty. Malice can be slow murder executed by insinuation, innuendo, injustice. Offense can be the slow poison through suspicion and slander that begins with character assassination and concludes with broken hearts. If anger has arisen, with or without justification, we are not to "let the sun go down upon [our] wrath: Neither give place to the devil" (Ephesians 4:26, 27).

If the wrong is against us, then we are to forgive. We are

taught to pray: "Forgive us our debts, as we forgive our debtors." The explanation is given by the Saviour: "For if ye forgive men their trespasses, your heavenly Father will also forgive you: But if ye forgive not men their trespasses, neither will your Father forgive your trespasses" (Matthew 6:14, 15). By some it is alleged that this is legalism. No, it is, rather, life, spiritual life.

The prayer of faith is an impossibility without that kind of forgiveness.

> And when ye stand praying, forgive, if ye have ought against any: that your Father also which is in heaven may forgive your trespasses. But if ye do not forgive, neither will your Father which is in heaven forgive your trespasses (Mark 11:25, 26).

James 5:16 elaborates that teaching in saying: "Confess your faults one to another, and pray one for another, that ye may be healed. The effectual fervent prayer of a righteous man availeth much."

The extent of forgiveness is unlimited. When Peter inquired, "Lord, how oft shall my brother sin against me, and I forgive him? till seven times?" the Saviour replied, "I say not unto thee, until seven times: but until seventy times seven" (Matthew 18: 21, 22). The intent is not that we should keep an accurate account of the number of times we forgive an individual, but rather that forgiveness is to be boundless. The Saviour Himself at Calvary prayed, "Father, forgive them for they know not what they do." Because of His love and sacrifice for us we have forgiveness and therefore we are taught:

> Grieve not the holy Spirit of God, whereby ye are sealed unto the day of redemption. Let all bitterness, and wrath, and anger, and clamour, and evil speaking, be put away from you, with all malice: And be ye kind one to another, tenderhearted, forgiving one another, even as God for Christ's sake hath forgiven you (Ephesians 4:30-32).

If the injury and injustice has been on our part, then we are to make the move immediately for reconciliation with the offended one. The Saviour said that when there comes to our remembrance that a brother has something against us we are to leave whatever we are doing, even prayer and service for God, and be first reconciled to our brother in Christ. Without restoration of that fellowship communion with God is an impossibility. We cannot be reconciled to God without being first reconciled to our brother. We cannot honor God by worship and work until we have humbled ourselves to ask forgiveness of another. True prayer involves prior penitence on our part, for, "If I regard iniquity in my heart, the Lord will not hear me" (Psalm 66:18). First things must come first, and the Lord Jesus taught plainly that first we are to be reconciled to our brother and then come to God.

In experience we learn that almost always reconciliation is achieved when two who have been estranged meet face to face with openness of heart and earnest desire for the Lord's glory. Such a meeting of hearts bring tears of reconciliation and joy, followed by the freedom of the Holy Spirit. A whole congregation or school or mission society or whatever Christian work is involved can be blessed by restoration of understanding, unity and harmony.

The reconciliation should be sought immediately even as the Lord Jesus said, "Agree with thine adversary quickly, whilest thou art in the way" (Matthew 5:25). There is the pertinent admonition in Hebrews 12:14, 15 which gives us instruction and exhortation to "Follow peace with all men, and holiness, without which no man shall see the Lord: looking diligently lest any man fail of the grace of God; lest any root of bitterness springing up trouble you, and thereby many be defiled." Thereby we walk in the light and not in darkness, in freedom of heart and not in bondage of bitterness. After we have left our worship *there* in the place of prayer and have had fellowship restored with our brother in Christ, *then* we can return to our worship and our work for God will be blessed.

26

THEN shall thy light break forth

Cry aloud, spare not, lift up thy voice like a trumpet, and shew my people their transgressions, and the house of Jacob their sins. Yet they seek me daily, and delight to know my ways, as a nation that did righteousness, and forsook not the ordinance of their God: they ask of me the ordinances of justice; they take delight in approaching to God.

Wherefore have we fasted, say they, and thou seest not? wherefore have we afflicted our soul, and thou takest no knowledge? Behold, in the day of your fast ye find pleasure, and exact all your labours. Behold, ye fast for strife and debate, and to smite with the fist of wickedness: ye shall not fast as ye do this day, to make your voice to be heard on high. Is it such a fast that I have chosen? a day for a man to afflict his soul? is it to bow down his head as a bulrush, and to spread sackcloth and ashes under him? wilt thou call this a fast, and an acceptable day to the LORD? Is not this the fast that I have chosen? to loose the bands of wickedness, to undo the heavy burdens, and to let the oppressed go free, and that ye break every yoke? Is it not to deal thy bread to the hungry, and that thou bring the poor that are cast out to thy house? when thou seest the naked, that thou cover him; and that thou hide not thyself from thine own flesh?

Then shall thy light break forth as the morning, and thine health shall spring forth speedily: and thy righteousness shall go before thee: the glory of the LORD shall be thy rereward. Then shalt thou

call, and the Lord shall answer; thou shalt cry, and he shall say,
Here I am. . . .   — Isaiah 58:1-9

Then shall thy light break forth as the morning, and thine health
shall spring forth speedily . . . *then* shalt thou call and the Lord shall
answer . . .   — Isaiah 58:8, 9

HYPOCRISY of any kind is a sham and a sufficient cause for
shamefulness. The Lord Jesus had far more criticism for the
self-satisfied and sophisticated Pharisees who were hypocrites
than for the publicans who were out and out sinners and who
made no pretense to being anything but what they really were.
At the beginning of His ministry, as He taught the multitudes on
the mountainside, the Saviour said:

> Take heed that ye do not your alms before men, to be seen of them:
> otherwise ye have no reward of your Father which is in heaven.
> Therefore when thou doest thine alms, do not sound a trumpet be-
> fore thee, as the hypocrites do in the synagogues and in the streets,
> that they may have glory of men. Verily I say unto you, They have
> their reward. But when thou doest alms, let not thy left hand know
> what thy right hand doeth: That thine alms may be in secret: and
> thy Father which seeth in secret himself shall reward thee openly.
> And when thou prayest, thou shalt not be as the hypocrites are: for
> they love to pray standing in the synagogues and in the corners of
> the streets, that they may be seen of men. Verily I say unto you,
> They have their reward (Matthew 6:1-5).

Toward the end of His ministry He believed it to be necessary to speak out again as He had done frequently in the past
against the "play-acting" of the scribes and Pharisees. He spoke
pointedly and with pain I am sure:

> Woe unto you, scribes and Pharisees, hypocrites! for ye devour
> widows' houses, and for a pretence make long prayer: therefore ye
> shall receive the greater damnation. . . . Woe unto you, scribes and
> Pharisees, hypocrites! for ye pay tithe of mint and anise and cummin,
> and have omitted the weightier matters of the law, judgment, mercy,
> and faith: these ought ye to have done, and not to leave the other
> undone. Ye blind guides, which strain at a gnat, and swallow a
> camel. Woe unto you, scribes and Pharisees, hypocrites! for ye make
> clean the outside of the cup and of the platter, but within they are
> full of extortion and excess. Thou blind Pharisee, cleanse first that
> which is within the cup and platter, that the outside of them may
> be clean also. Woe unto you, scribes and Pharisees, hypocrites! for

> ye are like unto whited sepulchres, which indeed appear beautiful outward, but are within full of dead men's bones, and of all uncleanness. Even so ye also outwardly appear righteous unto men, but within ye are full of hypocrisy and iniquity (Matthew 23:14, 23-28).

Hypocrisy has always been hateful to God, and is despised by mankind as well. Hypocrisy is readily rationalized by those who make pretense, especially in matters of religion. Just as was true in the days of the Lord Jesus that those who appeared to men to be the most religious were in actuality hypocrites, just so it was in the time of Isaiah the prophet. God said to him that his people abounded in transgressions, yet outwardly they went to the temple, kept their religious duties punctiliously, especially the keeping of fast days required by the law of Moses. In actuality their inner motivation was greediness and wickedness, for the prophet pointed out to them, "Behold, ye fast for strife and debate, and to smite with the fist of wickedness: ye shall not fast as ye do this day, to make your voice to be heard on high" (Isaiah 58:4).

The same was later true of the Pharisees of whom our Lord said:

> Moreover, when ye fast, be not, as the hypocrites, of a sad countenance: for they disfigure their faces, that they may appear unto men to fast. Verily I say unto you, They have their reward. But thou, when thou fastest, anoint thine head, and wash thy face; that thou appear not unto men to fast, but unto thy Father which is in secret: and thy Father, which seeth in secret, shall reward thee openly (Matthew 6:16-18).

Throughout the Scriptures, fasting, implying an abstinence from food so that the individual might devote himself wholly to the worship of God, is clearly taught. The Lord Jesus Himself and His disciples observed times of fasting, but not to the same extent as did John the Baptist and his disciples. Moses spent forty days and nights before the Lord on Mount Horeb, much as did the Lord Jesus in the days of His temptation in the wilderness. The Psalmist spoke of fasting on behalf of his friends who were ill (Psalm 35:13); Daniel did so under deep exercise of soul and received special revelations from the Most High (Daniel 9:3), as did the Apostle Paul who encouraged the practice (I Corinthians 7:5; II Corinthians 6:5; 11:27).

167

But fasting, as with other religious exercises, can be only a form and without spiritual benefit. The true fast results in righteous living, and this is the fasting that pleases the Lord, as He said:

> Is not this the fast that I have chosen? to loose the bands of wickedness, to undo the heavy burdens, and to let the oppressed go free, and that ye break every yoke? Is it not to deal thy bread to the hungry, and that thou bring the poor that are cast out to thy house? when thou seest the naked, that thou cover him; and that thou hide not thyself from thine own flesh? (Isaiah 58:6, 7).

Abstinence from necessities should make us increasingly aware of the need of our fellow men. We need to have both solitude and service, both time for prayer behind the shut door and time for helpfulness to others with an open door. Both can be an expression of a true fast in the sight of God.

There are times when God calls us to be entirely alone with Himself, and to that call we are to be implicitly obedient. There is the warning of the Saviour, however, not to call attention to the fact that we are giving ourselves to prayer and fasting lest we evoke, perhaps quite unwittingly, commendation of our spirituality. Then we have reward of men and no reward from the Faithful One who has called us to fasting.

There are other times when we are under deep exercise of soul, and the answer from God is to be found in the fast that is marked by faithful helpfulness to others. The late Dr. Albert Benjamin Simpson, founder of the Christian and Missionary Alliance, told of an occasion when he gave himself to prayer and fasting so as to know the will of God regarding a great decision. All day long there seemed to be no answer. Toward evening he remembered a family, recently bereaved of the father, who needed the help of the pastor. Reluctantly leaving his study he went to the sorrowing widow and children, and in a matter of a few minutes of helpfulness to them his own need of guidance was wonderfully supplied. The promise is, "*Then* shall thy light break forth as the morning," and continues in verse 11, "And the Lord shall guide thee continually."

There are occasions when the obvious self-will and selfishness of others may seem to interfere with our prayer life or our service for God. Even then a constructive attitude on our part can overrule that handicap. Years ago a schoolmate of Mrs. Edman came to our home for a visit. By Saturday evening both my wife and two of our small sons were ill with influenza. I had preaching engagements the next day in that New England community and was grateful for the help our friend could give in the home. However, early on Sunday morning she decided she just had to go home. A quiet request for helpfulness to us in our need was wholly ignored. Leaving the home in charge of just a little boy I took our "friend" to the railroad station, which was a long way out of my way. But as she boarded the train who should be arriving but some neighbors of ours returning from the funeral of a son in West Virginia. Right there the Lord gave opportunity to minister the Word to them, with resultant blessing in their hearts and home.

Helpfulness to others irrespective of their attitude can constitute the true fast which results in light for our path, health and strength for our service, God's presence and protection with us, and His answer to our prayer.

27

THEN shalt thou delight

If thou turn away thy foot from the sabbath, from doing thy pleasure
on my holy day; and call the sabbath a delight, the holy of the Lord,
honourable; and shalt honour him, not doing thine own ways, nor
finding thine own pleasure, nor speaking thine own words: Then
shalt thou delight thyself in the Lord; and I will cause thee to ride
upon the high places of the earth, and feed thee with the heritage
of Jacob thy father: for the mouth of the Lord hath spoken it.
— Isaiah 58:13, 14

Then shalt thou delight thyself in the Lord . . . — Isaiah 58:14

THE keeping of the Lord's day is an accurate criterion of the
level of spiritual life of an individual or of a nation. The keeping
of the Sabbath on the part of Israel is given in much detail in
the Old Testament. While the details of Sabbath keeping as
stated in the law, which was the "schoolmaster to bring us to
Christ," are not pertinent to the New Testament dispensation,
the basic principles of Sabbath keeping should prevail.

The divine principle of the Sabbath is that God established
the seven-day week and that one day in seven should be set
aside for worship and rest. In the account of creation we read:

Thus the heavens and the earth were finished, and all the host of
them. And on the seventh day God ended his work which he had

171

made; and he rested on the seventh day from all his work which he had made. And God blessed the seventh day, and sanctified it: because that in it he had rested from all his work which God created and made (Genesis 2:1-3).

The divine provision was not one day in five or ten or any other number except seven. Without doubt this was understood by the patriarchs of old, such as Abraham, Isaac and Jacob. Apparently it became forgotten by their descendants because before the Law was given to Moses there was the reminder to Israel, recently come out of Egypt, that "tomorrow is the rest of the holy Sabbath unto the Lord" (Exodus 16:23). This reminder was given in connection with the gathering of the manna which was available only on six days in the week. When the Law was given the Decalogue stated (Exodus 20:8-11):

Remember the sabbath day, to keep it holy. Six days shalt thou labour, and do all thy work: But the seventh day is the sabbath of the Lord thy God: in it thou shalt not do any work, thou, nor thy son, nor thy daughter, thy manservant, nor thy maidservant, nor thy cattle, nor thy stranger that is within thy gates: For in six days the Lord made heaven and earth, the sea, and all that in them is, and rested the seventh day: wherefore the Lord blessed the sabbath day, and hallowed it.

The Law was given expressly to Israel. The Sabbath was designed by God to be a sign between Himself, the Creator, and Israel whom He sanctified (Exodus 31:12-17). It was likewise to be a weekly reminder that they had been bond slaves in the land of Egypt and that the Lord their God brought them out "through a mighty hand and by a stretched out arm"; therefore the Lord commanded them "to keep the sabbath day" (Deuteronomy 5:15).

In New Testament days, the first day of the week became the day of worship and rest to be observed by Christians, because of the resurrection of Jesus Christ on the first day of the week and the beginning of the New Covenant. Every Old Testament feast that was symbolical of the coming Christian era was on the first day of the week, as the Feast of First Fruits (Leviticus 23:11) and the Day of Pentecost (Leviticus 23:15, 16). Just as blessing was promised to Israel in the keeping of the

172

Sabbath, the same principle applies to Christians in the proper keeping of the Lord's day.

"*Then* shalt thou delight thyself in the Lord . . ." This promise in God's Word came to me early in my Christian life. Shortly after returning home from overseas service in the First World War and enrolling at the University of Illinois, I was reading through *Isaiah* for the first time. This passage in the fifty-eighth chapter stood out before me as a challenge. I had noticed that it was the practice of all the fellows in the house where I lived to study all day Sunday. Saturday afternoon and evening seemed wholly given to doing their own desires, and there was little reverence or respect for the Lord's day.

It seemed to me that God was saying that if I would do my part in the keeping of His day that He would do His part. I could understand verse 13 for its language seemed perfectly clear. The condition read, "Speak thou also unto the children of Israel, saying, Verily my sabbaths ye shall keep: for it is a sign between me and you throughout your generations; that ye may know that I am the LORD that doth sanctify you" (Exodus 31:13). The Lord's day was to be a delight and a day dedicated to Him in which I was to do His pleasure and not mine. (I did have good example in my home background for there the family kept the Lord's day holy, separate from other days in the week.) Then and there I made a covenant to keep the Lord's day separate from secular duties (from study in particular), with difference to dress and deportment on that day. God's Word and work and worship should predominate throughout the day.

I found that I could fulfill all responsibilities that came upon me during six days with the result that there was no need or desire to cheat on the Lord by taking part or whole of His day. It was to be sure, necessary to budget my time carefully. I learned that it was helpful to get all my studies and other duties completed by Saturday evening so that there could be a time of preparation for the Lord's day to follow. Thereupon began the practice of rising on Sunday morning for devotional reading of the Word rather than sleeping in because of being out late the night before. Thus the Lord's day became a delight, as the Scripture said, a day "to honor Him." It became the occasion

173

for unhurried fellowship with Him in the private place of prayer and in His house of worship. The Lord's day became a reminder that He is risen indeed!

Over the years my wife and I have sought not only to keep the Lord's day ourselves but also to teach the lads in our home and the people of God in the college and in the church to do so. We, as a family, have found the Lord's day to be a delight, a rest and a re-creation.

Just what the remainder of God's promise in verse 14 means I am not sure, but it states a principle, I believe, of what God will bring to pass in any life that obeys His injunction regarding the keeping of His day. The Word says, ". . . and I will cause thee to ride upon the high places of the earth, and feed thee with the heritage of Jacob thy father: for the mouth of the LORD hath spoken it." I believe it and leave it with Him who made the promise. God has His own way of causing His promises faithfully and fully to come to pass.

God Holds the Key

God holds the key of all unknown,
  And I am glad;
If other hands should hold the key,
Or if He trusted it to me,
  I might be sad.

What if tomorrow's cares were here
  Without its rest!
I'd rather He unlocked the day;
And, as the hours swing open, say,
  "My will is best."

The very dimness of my sight
  Makes me secure;
For, groping in my misty way,
I feel His hand; I hear Him say,
  "My help is sure."

I cannot read His future plans;
  But this I know:
I have the smiling of His face,
And all the refuge of His grace,
  While here below.

Enough! this covers all my wants,
  And so I rest!
For what I cannot, He can see,
And in His care I saved shall be,
  For ever blest.

— J. PARKER

28

Even THERE shall thy hand lead me

O Lord, thou hast searched me, and known me. Thou knowest my downsitting and mine uprising, thou understandest my thought afar off. Thou compassest my path and my lying down, and art acquainted with all my ways. For there is not a word in my tongue, but, lo, O Lord, thou knowest it altogether. Thou hast beset me behind and before, and laid thine hand upon me. Such knowledge is too wonderful for me; it is high, I cannot attain unto it. Whither shall I go from thy spirit? or whither shall I flee from thy presence? If I ascend up into heaven, thou art there: if I make my bed in hell, behold, thou art there. If I take the wings of the morning, and dwell in the uttermost parts of the sea; even there shall thy hand lead me, and thy right hand shall hold me. If I say, Surely the darkness shall cover me; even the night shall be light about me. Yea, the darkness hideth not from thee; but the night shineth as the day: the darkness and the light are both alike to thee.   — Psalm 139:1-12

. . . even *there* shall thy hand lead me, and thy right hand shall hold me.   — Psalm 139:10

TO bolster his unbelief and to make it known to others, an atheist made for himself a motto, "God is nowhere." He cut out large letters and attached them to the wall over his desk. One day a gust of wind blew some of them down and his young daughter, eager to be of help, replaced them for her father; but in so doing she caused the motto to read, "God is now here." The letters were the same but the meaning was diametrically opposed to the original. The atheist and the theist have the same facts — the universe, which is God's general revelation, and the Bible, which is His special revelation — and the interpretation thereof depends entirely upon the individual.

For the believer there may be matters little understood, or not at all, but with Whittier he can say:

> I know not where His islands
> Lift their fronded palms in air,
> I only know I cannot drift
> Beyond His love and care.

God's presence with His people wherever they may be should be a reality increasingly wonderful to them. King David knew that reality and therefore he could sing, "I have set the Lord always before me; because he is at my right hand, I shall not be moved. Therefore my heart is glad, and my glory rejoiceth: my flesh also shall rest in hope" (Psalm 16:8, 9).

The Saviour gave assurance to us that He would be with us all the days even to the end of the age (Matthew 28:20). To Moses the word was, "My presence shall go with thee, and I will give thee rest" (Exodus 33:14). At the close of his days, Moses, that man of God, reminded Joshua, and all of God's people all down the ages for that matter, that "the Lord, he it is that doth go before thee; he will be with thee, he will not fail thee, neither forsake thee: fear not, neither be dismayed" (Deuteronomy 31:8). That promise is repeated and amplified in Hebrews 13:5, 6 which declares, "Let your conversation be without covetousness; and be content with such things as ye have: for he hath said, I will never leave thee, nor forsake thee. So that we may boldly say, The Lord is my helper, and I will not fear what man shall do unto me."

In Psalm 139, David sought words in which to express the reality of God's presence. He realized that God knew him altogether, his downsitting and uprising, even all his thoughts and his ways. In contemplating such omniscience of the Most High he could only say, "Thou hast beset me behind and before, and laid thine hand upon me. Such knowledge is too wonderful for me; it is high, I cannot attain unto it" (Psalm 139:5, 6).

In the light of such knowledge on the part of the Almighty why should we ever be tempted to think that He does not know the circumstances in which we find ourselves at a given moment? He uses the fathomless infinity of His creation to measure His concern and care for us. In His Word He assures us that "as the heaven is high above the earth, so great is his mercy toward them that fear him. As far as the east is from the west, so far hath he removed our transgressions from us" (Psalm 103:11, 12). Who can estimate the height of heaven? How far is east from west? What measures of the magnitude of God's mercy and forgiveness are these!

The same thought was expressed eloquently through the prophet Isaiah. He pointed to the immensity of the universe and then inquired as to how anyone could say that his way is hid from the Almighty. This is the word God gave through him:

> To whom then will ye liken me, or shall I be equal? saith the Holy One. Lift up your eyes on high, and behold who hath created these things, that bringeth out their host by number: he calleth them all by names by the greatness of his might, for that he is strong in power; not one faileth. Why sayest thou, O Jacob, and speakest, O Israel, My way is hid from the LORD, and my judgment is passed over from my God? Hast thou not known? hast thou not heard, that the everlasting God, the LORD, the Creator of the ends of the earth, fainteth not, neither is weary? there is no searching of his understanding. He giveth power to the faint; and to them that have no might he increaseth strength. Even the youths shall faint and be weary, and the young men shall utterly fall: But they that wait upon the LORD shall renew their strength; they shall mount up with wings as eagles; they shall run, and not be weary; and they shall walk, and not faint (Isaiah 40:25-31).

It was in the light of such revelation that the Psalmist realized that God is everywhere. There was nowhere to flee from His presence, should one desire so to do, not in the heavenlies nor in the grave nor in the uttermost parts of the sea far beyond the horizon. Even *there* God's hand would hold him.

Even where? You and I face this question in times of doubt and darkness, in the days and nights of uncertainty when everything certain becomes dim and all that seemed to be nailed down begins to come loose. It is at the extremity of our endurance that we find God's grace to be sufficient for us and that our weakness becomes our strength. It is in the depths of despair that we find God to be there with His word of assurance and awareness of His presence. It is in the hour of greatest danger and even in the face of death that we realize vividly the divine presence.

Eddie Powell of Jacksonville, Florida, was perhaps the most badly wounded soldier lad of the many hundreds who went from Wheaton's campus to the battlefields of World War II. For us who had to remain behind and who could not be "re-treaded" for service in the Second War, there was the responsibility for earnest intercession in behalf of those who faced danger for us. We learned that Eddie had been wounded and was hospitalized in Britain. He was not returned to the States for a long time, and after that it was nearly two years before even his parents could visit him in an army hospital. In the good providence of God, Eddie was fully restored except for a slight limp, and returned to Wheaton before going out into the Lord's service. His testimony is given briefly in a little tract entitled, "He Was There." Given up for dead on the battlefield with body mangled almost beyond recognition, he was aware of His Saviour's presence, of the One who had assured him that He never leaves nor forsakes His own. Even *there* He was there.

It is even there that the child of God learns that "darkness hideth not from thee, but the night shineth as the day: the darkness and the light are both alike to thee" (Psalm 139:12).

Even *there*, just where you are right now, the Lord is with you.

29

And he blessed him THERE

And Jacob was left alone; and there wrestled a man with him until
the breaking of the day. And when he saw that he prevailed not
against him, he touched the hollow of his thigh; and the hollow of
Jacob's thigh was out of joint, as he wrestled with him. And he said,
Let me go, for the day breaketh. And he said, I will not let thee go,
except thou bless me. And he said unto him, What is thy name?
And he said, Jacob. And he said, Thy name shall be called no more
Jacob, but Israel: for as a prince hast thou power with God and with
men, and hast prevailed. And Jacob asked him, and said, Tell me,
I pray thee, thy name. And he said, Wherefore is it that thou dost
ask after my name? And he blessed him there. And Jacob called the
name of the place Peniel: for I have seen God face to face, and my
life is preserved.   — Genesis 32:24-30

And he blessed him *there*.   — Genesis 32:29

JACOB had come to the end of himself. The patriarch was by
this time an old man more than a hundred years of age, and for
a long time he had been coming to the crisis of utter abandonment to God. All his life long he had been a schemer, given to
sharp dealings always in his own favor. By cunning and crafti-
ness he had taken both birthright and paternal blessing from
Esau his older brother. For his own advantage he had deceived
his father and his father-in-law. It might have seemed that he

181

could go on successfully in his self-centeredness and scheming; but God knows when and where to bring a heart to the end of itself.

After long absence from his homeland, Jacob with his family and with his flocks and herds was en route to the place of his birth. He was returning under divine instruction, for the Most High had sent him the word: "I am the God of Bethel, where thou anointedst the pillar, and where thou vowedst a vow unto me: now arise, get thee out from this land, and return unto the land of thy kindred" (Genesis 31:13). Years before, Jacob had made a vow before the Almighty, saying:

> If God will be with me, and will keep me in this way that I go, and will give me bread to eat, and raiment to put on, so that I come again to my father's house in peace; then shall the LORD be my God: And this stone, which I have set for a pillar, shall be God's house: and of all that thou shalt give me I will surely give the tenth unto thee (Genesis 28:20-22).

God had made good His part of that vow; it seemed that all was well with Jacob. Then came the alarming news that his estranged brother Esau with a band of four hundred men was coming to meet the defenseless Jacob and his family. Jacob was

> greatly afraid and distressed: and he divided the people that was with him, and the flocks, and herds, and the camels, into two bands; and said, If Esau come to the one company, and smite it, then the other company which is left shall escape (Genesis 32:7, 8).

Accordingly, he sent over the brook Jabbok his flocks and herds, beginning with those that were least valuable, and finally he sent also his family.

"And Jacob was left alone . . ." (v. 24). All he had in the world, all he had gained for himself in one way or another, all was apparently lost. The morning sun would show the arrival of Esau and the capture of sheep and goats, cows and camels, and most of all the mothers and the children.

Alone with God, this was the crisis hour for Jacob.

What is the heart experience of a soul that is shut in with God, when the door to the world and all that one holds dear is closed? For Abraham it was on one occasion "an horror of great darkness" (Genesis 15:12). For Moses at the burning bush it was removal of shoes to indicate humbling of heart (Exodus 3:5). For Isaiah it was awareness of his sinfulness and unworthiness (6:5) and for Daniel, utter loss of strength. For Jacob it was wrestling with a Stranger until the breaking of the day. The outer exertion and determination were illustrative of the inner struggle of his soul. The death pangs of self wracked his being, for he was resisting God to the bitter end.

He came to that end at the breaking of day. He could struggle no longer, he could only cling to the Almighty and make his despairing plea, "I will not let thee go, except thou bless me" (v. 26).

"And he blessed him *there.*" Where? *There* marked the place of utter brokenness before God. To be sure, Jacob's thigh was out of place because of wrestling, but that physical factor was but the outer indication of his broken will. He admitted that his name was Jacob, meaning, "supplanter," "deceiver," "schemer." Of all of that he was heartily ashamed. *Then* his name was changed to Israel: "A prince of God," one to have "power with God and with men."

The place of brokenness was the place of blessing and of beginning again. Jacob had become Israel, "a prince with God." No longer was he Jacob, "the supplanter," the self-seeking, self-willed deceiver. What were the details of the blessing he experienced *there* we do not know? Jacob never explained it afterward. It was something between God and himself, something too deep and sacred for further statement, or even for formulation into words. The blessings of this experience he carried with him always. In years to come it was Jacob become Israel who blessed Pharaoh, the mightiest monarch of that day (Genesis 47:10), and who blessed his twelve sons (Genesis 49) as well as the two sons of Joseph (Genesis 48). Thereafter God was wont to call Himself by the name, "the God of Jacob" (Psalm 146:5).

"And he blessed him *there.*" He who is the same yesterday and today and forever still meets just *there* the heart of His child

183

who has come to the end of himself. Are you *there?* Has everything apparently failed and is your heart filled with fear of the future? Are you in utter helplessness and human hopelessness, alone with God and clinging to Him? Have you come to the place of utter yieldedness, of abandonment to Him? That place of bewilderment and brokenness is the place of blessing and of beginning a life that is new and full of peace and power.

30

THEN Hezekiah . . . rose early

Hezekiah began to reign when he was five and twenty years old, and he reigned nine and twenty years in Jerusalem. And his mother's name was Abijah, the daughter of Zechariah. And he did that which was right in the sight of the LORD, according to all that David his father had done.

He in the first year of his reign, in the first month, opened the doors of the house of the LORD, and repaired them. And he brought in the priests and the Levites, and gathered them together into the east street. And said unto them, Hear me, ye Levites, sanctify now yourselves, and sanctify the house of the LORD God of your fathers, and carry forth the filthiness out of the holy place, For our fathers have trespassed, and done that which was evil in the eyes of the LORD our God, and have forsaken him, and have turned away their faces from the habitation of the LORD, and turned their backs.

Then Hezekiah the king rose early, and gathered the rulers of the city, and went up to the house of the Lord. —II Chronicles 29:1-6, 20

Then Hezekiah the king rose early, and gathered the rulers of the city, and went up to the house of the LORD. —II Chronicles 29:20

A SHIP'S course is determined by the captain and not by the crew. The shepherd, not the sheep, determines in which field the flock will be pastured. The administration, not the students, determines the policies and standards of a college. The father, not the children, sets the pattern of life for the family.

The destiny of any group, be it large or small, a nation or a local church, or a little family, is dependent upon the decision of the leader. If he determines the program with decisiveness and determination, with insight and foresight, within the principles of divine revelation, the group goes forward under the blessing of God, irrespective of difficulties that may arise in the way.

The experience of Israel is recorded in the Scriptures to teach just such lessons. When the ruler rebelled against God and refused to walk in His ways, the people were led astray and the land suffered. For example, the father of Hezekiah, King Ahaz, "did not that which was right in the sight of the LORD, like David his father: for he walked in the ways of the kings of Israel, and made also molten images for Baalim" (II Chronicles 28:1, 2). As a result, idolatry abounded in the land and "the Lord brought Judah low because of Ahaz, king of Israel" (II Chronicles 28:19). The idols were "the ruin of him, and of all Israel" (II Chronicles 28:23).

Hezekiah, on the other hand, "did that which was right in the sight of the Lord, according to all that David his father [that is, his ancestor, the king of Israel] had done." The king took his stand for God and for the right, and although there were many difficulties during his long reign it is recorded of him that

> thus did Hezekiah throughout all Judah, and wrought that which was good and right and truth before the LORD his God. . . . in every work that he began in the service of the house of God, and in the law, and in the commandments, to seek his God, he did it with all his heart, and prospered (II Chronicles 31:20, 21).

Righteousness does exalt a nation, and such standards of uprightness in the fear of God are the responsibility of the leader. The pathway to progress and prosperity, spiritual and material, is set by the prince who walks with God and is obedient to His commands. Where he goes, others will follow.

Hezekiah started out right, for, "in the first year of his reign, in the first month, he opened the doors of the house of the Lord, and repaired them" (29:3). In all humility and genuine repentance he acknowledged that the previous generation had forsaken God. The Temple worship had been largely abandoned and

186

the house of the God neglected so that it was in disrepair as well as in disrepute. The first move was to re-establish worship and the place of worship. Said the king to the spiritual leaders of his land:

> Now it is in mine heart to make a covenant with the LORD God of Israel that his fierce wrath may turn away from us. My sons, be not now negligent: for the LORD hath chosen you to stand before him, to serve him, and that ye should minister unto him, and burn incense (II Chronicles 29:10, 11).

As a result, they set out to prepare themselves for worship as well as to repair the house of God. Their king was a real leader and they would be loyal to him.

The king knew how to delegate responsibility, a secret not understood by every leader of men. He gave specific assignments to certain men for the Temple work and they in turn had others help them. It was Dwight L. Moody who said that it is better to get ten men to work than for one man to do the work of ten.

Teamwork consists of leadership on the one hand and loyalty on the other, of executive ability and excellent attitude, of understanding and enthusiasm, of command and cooperation. With their assignment made clear, the Levites leaped with alacrity into action and within a week the Temple had been cleansed. There is a great truth in that word of Psalm 110:3, "Thy people shall be willing in the day of thy power." Whereas in times of spiritual decline there may be irresponsibility and unresponsiveness to leadership, in the day when God's power is manifest in the life of the leader the people are willing for any sacrifice or assignment that will achieve the purpose of God.

Sometimes an administrator faces an unhappy and unwholesome situation. In that case he should read the ninth and tenth chapters of the Book of Ezra. When the leader learned the sad spiritual and moral conditions of his people, he was overwhelmed. His first reaction was properly to pray and to make confession before Him who is faithful to hear and to forgive. When he had thus prayed with tears, many of his people gathered together and likewise became deeply concerned. To Ezra they said, "Arise, for this matter belongeth unto thee: we also will be with thee:

be of good courage, and do it" (Ezra 10:4). Prayer followed by faithful cooperation of one's assistants and also by plain speaking can resolve problems that are too great in themselves for the leader.

To return to Hezekiah, we observe that after the Levites in obedience to the example and instructions of their monarch had made ready the Temple, "*then* Hezekiah the king rose early, and gathered the rulers of the city, and went up to the house of God" (29:20). The time for worship had come, now that the work had been completed. The king himself was present to observe that all was done according to divine instructions and he was active in encouraging the Levites to do their part faithfully. As a result, "they sang praises with gladness, and they bowed their heads and worshipped" (v. 30). When people are glad-hearted there is little limit as to what they can do in the service of God.

As a result of the king's leadership and the Levites' cooperation, the people responded with gladness of heart and gratitude to God. They "brought in sacrifices and thank offerings, and as many as were of a free heart burnt offerings" (v. 31). There were so many that the Lord's servants in the Temple were overwhelmed. The ensuing prosperity of the kingdom followed as a natural consequence.

The account goes on to say:

> And as soon as the commandment came abroad, the children of Israel brought in abundance the firstfruits of corn, wine, and oil, and honey, and of all the increase of the field; and the tithe of all things brought they in abundantly. . . . And when Hezekiah and the princes came and saw the heaps, they blessed the LORD, and his people Israel. Then Hezekiah questioned with the priests and the Levites concerning the heaps. And Azariah the chief priest of the house of Zadok answered him, and said, Since the people began to bring the offerings into the house of the LORD, we have had enough to eat, and have left plenty: for the LORD hath blessed his people; and that which is left is this great store (II Chronicles 31:5, 8-10).

Thus if leadership takes its stand others will stand also. If the leader loves God and honors Him, others will follow in ways of righteousness.

God Moves in a Mysterious Way

God moves in a mysterious way
   His wonders to perform;
He plants His footsteps in the sea,
   And rides upon the storm.

Deep in unfathomable mines
   Of never-failing skill,
He treasures up His bright designs,
   And works His sovereign will.

Ye fearful saints, fresh courage take!
   The clouds ye so much dread
Are big with mercy, and will break
   In blessings on your head.

Judge not the Lord by feeble sense,
   But trust Him for His grace;
Behind a frowning providence
   He hides a smiling face.

His purposes will ripen fast,
   Unfolding every hour;
The bud may have a bitter taste,
   But sweet will be the flower.

Blind unbelief is sure to err,
   And scan His work in vain;
God is His own interpreter,
   And He will make it plain.

— WILLIAM COWPER

31

THEN shall the lord

But when the Philistines heard that they had anointed David king over Israel, all the Philistines came up to seek David; and David heard of it, and went down to the hold. The Philistines also came and spread themselves in the valley of Rephaim. And David enquired of the LORD, saying, Shall I go up to the Philistines? wilt thou deliver them into mine hand? And the LORD said unto David, Go up: for I will doubtless deliver the Philistines into thine hand. And David came to Baal-perazim, and David smote them there, and said, The LORD hath broken forth upon mine enemies before me, as the breach of waters. Therefore he called the name of that place Baal-perazim. And there they left their images, and David and his men burned them.

And the Philistines came up yet again, and spread themselves in the valley of Rephaim. And when David enquired of the LORD, he said, Thou shalt not go up, but fetch a compass behind them and come upon them over against the mulberry trees. And let it be, when thou hearest the sound of a going in the tops of the mulberry trees, that then thou shalt bestir thyself: for then shall the LORD go out before thee, to smite the host of the Philistines. And David did so, as the LORD had commanded him; and smote the Philistines from Geba until thou come to Gazer.   ——II Samuel 5:17-25

Then shall the LORD go out before thee . . .   — II Samuel 5:24

191

THE Almighty employs the extent of the universe to give us an estimate of how much more excellent are His ways than ours. This truth He emphasized in Isaiah 55:9, "For as the heavens are higher than the earth, so are my ways higher than your ways, and my thoughts than your thoughts."

Happy is the heart that is desirous of learning God's ways so as to walk in them. Such was David, as we observe in his life story and in his prayers. An example is found in Psalm 143:8-12:

> Cause me to hear thy lovingkindness in the morning; for in thee do
> I trust: cause me to know the way wherein I should walk; for I lift
> up my soul unto thee. Teach me to do thy will . . . lead me . . .
> quicken me. . . .

To hear God's loving kindness, to know the way he should take, to be taught His way, to be led in paths of righteousness, to be kept alert to the presence of the Holy One — such were the deep petitions of David's heart, and they should also be ours.

When he first became king over all twelve tribes of Israel, David learned that his inveterate foes, the Philistines, were on the march against him. He was no captain to call for retreat or compromise; rather, he rallied his forces and went out to meet the enemy. Although he was an experienced combat soldier he did not presume to order the battle on the basis of past experience. He made, instead, earnest inquiry of the Lord as to whether he should go against the Philistines and whether or not the Lord would give victory. In response to his inquiry the Most High gave His instructions, "Go up: for I will doubtless deliver the Philistines into thine hand" (v. 19). The result was a resounding victory.

The reality of asking guidance of God is written often in the Scriptures, Old Testament and New. Again and again God's people called upon Him for instruction and help, and the Faithful One answered their petitions. The teaching of the Scriptures is summarized succinctly and pointedly in James 1:2-8:

> My brethren, count it all joy when ye fall into divers temptations;
> knowing this, that the trying of your faith worketh patience. But let
> patience have her perfect work, that ye may be perfect and entire,
> wanting nothing. If any of you lack wisdom, let him ask of God,
> that giveth to all men liberally, and unbraideth not; and it shall be

given him. But let him ask in faith, nothing wavering. For he that wavereth is like a wave of the sea driven with the wind and tossed. For let not that man think that he shall receive any thing of the Lord. A double minded man is unstable in all his ways.

Of course, God's people will come to times of testing, and in these we learn patience to see what God will do and how He will answer prayer. We are to ask in faith for guidance without being double minded, that is, to think maybe yes or maybe no as far as God's provision for us. Like David and many others, of whom the Bible gives record, we are to pray, and in response to our prayer of faith God will provide the wisdom that we need.

One victory, however, does not mean that we have won the war over Satan and all his demonic host. Just as the Philistines came again against David, so our mortal foe will reappear with determination to destroy us or at least divert us from all the will of God. We are not to be ignorant of his devices. You will recall that Christian had the dreadful conflict with Apollyon just beyond Forgetful Green. We are ever to watch and to pray as well as to have on all the armor of God for in the moment of carelessness or spiritual conceit there may be unexpected conflict with the Wicked One.

As far as David could determine, the situation was precisely the same as in the previous battle: the Philistines were in the valley of Rephaim. All he had to do was to follow the tactics in the previous encounter and realize a similar victory. But that he did not do. Again he made request of the Most High for His guidance and help.

Presumption on our part is always the height of folly. Whereas it has been our experience to win a great victory by the guidance and grace of God, we are not to presume that we are to follow exactly the same procedure when next we come into similar circumstances of conflict. David knew that the Philistines were not stupid soldiers. They would reason that David's army would follow the previous plan of battle, and without doubt they had prepared thoroughly against that eventuality. The same method might succeed or might fail; therefore, David needed new instructions.

God's ways are not limited to our finite understanding. He knows the end of a given matter from the beginning and can give us wisdom far beyond our understanding of a given situation. Our safety lies in a sensitivity to His will, a tenderness of heart and a teachableness of spirit that is willing for any way that God should choose. That David had learned this lesson is obvious from his statement of experience recorded in Psalm 25:9 — "The meek will he guide in judgment: and the meek will he teach his way."

God's way is always higher and better than our way as heaven is high above the earth. Our part is to ask wisdom and then to be willing for God to show us another way, an untried tactic, a maneuver unfamiliar to ourselves and also to our foe.

The divine directions were explicit:

> Thou shalt not go up; but fetch a compass behind them, and come upon them over against the mulberry trees. And let it be, when thou hearest the sound of a going in the tops of the mulberry trees, that then thou shalt bestir thyself: for then shall the Lord go out before thee, to smite the host of the Philistines (II Samuel 5:23, 24).

Instead of a frontal attack, for which the Philistines would undoubtedly fully prepare, David and his men were to make an encircling movement which would bring them on the flanks of the enemy, the place where his forces were the weakest. As the result of David's implicit obedience to his Captain, his army won another resounding victory.

Like David, there are occasions when we have asked wisdom of God that we have to be willing to walk and work in an untried way, and be willing for an indefinite wait *until* there is clear indication from God to go forward. Not everyone can stand that test of patience after full preparedness has been made. King Saul, David's predecessor, could not wait until Samuel had come to have prayer for the armies of Israel; rather, the king himself entered presumptuously into the priest's office, with disastrous consequences. As a result, Samuel, who came in good time, had to say:

> Thou hast done foolishly: thou hast not kept the commandment of the Lord thy God, which he commanded thee: for now would the

Lord have established thy kingdom upon Israel for ever. But now thy kingdom shall not continue: the Lord hath sought him a man after his own heart, and the Lord hath commanded him to be captain over his people, because thou hast not kept that which the Lord commanded thee (I Samuel 13:13, 14).

Today's faithful preparation, prayer of faith and unfailing patience will provide tomorrow's triumph.

32

They watched him THERE

And when they had platted a crown of thorns, they put it upon his head, and a reed in his right hand: and they bowed the knee before him, and mocked him, saying, Hail, King of the Jews! And they spit upon him, and took the reed, and smote him on the head. And after that they had mocked him, they took the robe off from him, and put his own raiment on him, and led him away to crucify him. And as they came out, they found a man of Cyrene, Simon by name: him they compelled to bear his cross. And when they were come unto a place called Golgotha, that is to say, a place of a skull, they gave him vinegar to drink mingled with gall: and when he had tasted thereof, he would not drink. And they crucified him, and parted his garments, casting lots: that it might be fulfilled which was spoken by the prophet, They parted my garments among them, and upon my vesture did they cast lots. And sitting down they watched him *there*.   — Matthew 27:29-36

And sitting down they watched him *there*.   — Matthew 27:36

CALVARY was an unspeakably dreadful place!

Calvary marked the culmination of man's sinfulness, of his self-centeredness, self-sufficiency, of his actual hatred for God. The enmity against the Almighty had been building up over the centuries, as told by the Saviour in the parable of the vineyard and its keepers.

197

The owner of the vineyard repeatedly had sent his servants to receive the fruits of the vineyard, only to have some driven away, some stoned and others slain. At last the owner had sent his only son with the expectation that he would be respected and revered; but when the men saw him they said, "This is the heir; come, let us kill him, and let us seize on his inheritance" (Matthew 21:38). This they did after they had caught him and cast him out of the vineyard.

The Pharisees understood our Lord's parable to be concerning them, and instead of taking heed thereto they sought to lay hands on Him with the view of having Him slain, much as He Himself had foretold in the parable.

Calvary is not only the nadir of man's wickedness and willfulness but it is also the zenith of God's highest will and expression of His love for the wayward sons of men. The cross was not an afterthought for the Most High. He planned it before the foundation of the world.

Anyone reading the story for the first time would have the natural impression that Jesus of Nazareth had suffered more than enough, and without cause to be sure, before He was brought to Calvary. All that had preceded the actual crucifixion had been dreadful: the betrayal by Judas, the abandonment by His disciples and the denial by Peter, the trials before the elders of His people (wholly illegal at night by their own law) and those before Pilate and Herod, the mocking of the rude soldiery in the guard room, and the horrifying scourging inflicted upon the Saviour. The leather lash was studded with pieces of lead or other metal and the prisoner, stripped to the waist, was beaten mercilessly. Often the flesh of such victims was torn from the body, the eyes and the teeth knocked out, and not infrequently the prisoner died under the scourging. The prophet Isaiah, looking down the centuries by the Holy Spirit, spoke of the Saviour saying, ". . . his visage was so marred more than any man, and his form more than the sons of men" (Isaiah 52:14).

Thereafter came Calvary and its awful cross, the nailing of the hands and feet, the body propped up by a rude wooden peg which served as a seat of torture. Then the soldiers sat down to watch Him there. The watching implied both guarding Him, and the two other victims, lest there be any interference with the execution of the crucifixion, and also that they observed and heard all that took place.

The soldiers watched Him *there*. They were accustomed to such responsibilities, and utterly calloused against human suffering. They were entitled to the few possessions the three crucified men might own and therefore they divided such spoils by gambling for them. They saw and heard those who stood round about, the crowd that passed by and the company of priests that stood close enough to the cross to taunt the dying Son of God. Something about the scene, and especially its conclusion with an earthquake and the darkness, made a deep impression upon the soldiers so that their officer could only say, "Truly this was the Son of God" (Matthew 27:54)!

Two thieves were *there*, crucified with Him, "one on the right hand, and another on the left" (Matthew 27:38) fulfilling Isaiah 53:12.

Friends and followers of the Lord Jesus were *there*. The account relates that "many women were there beholding afar off, which followed Jesus from Galilee, ministering unto him; Among which was Mary Magdalene, and Mary the mother of James and Joses, and the mother of Zebedee's children" (Matthew 27:55, 56).

His own mother had come close enough to the cross to hear Him say that He was entrusting her to John the beloved disciple, at which time she was led away to John's home within the city. We can little fathom the horror and the helplessness of these faithful women who loved the Saviour. They with other disciples could not help but become utterly bewildered as well as deeply wounded of heart, for they had trusted that He was their Messiah to redeem Israel.

The foes of the Lord Jesus were *there*. Of course the rabble was present, the careless and the casual who attended such occasions out of sheer indifference to human suffering, much as we have the record of the medieval crowds that gathered to witness a public hanging or beheading.

And to our amazement, the religious leaders were *there*. They entered into the taunts of the coarse crowd, for the record goes on to say:

199

> Likewise also the chief priests mocking him, with the scribes and elders, said, He saved others; himself he cannot save. If he be the King of Israel, let him now come down from the cross, and we will believe him. He trusted in God; let him deliver him now, if he will have him: for he said, I am the Son of God (Matthew 27:41-43).

They should have been men of compassion because they professed to know God and serve Him; but the long history of mankind shows none so cruel as those who profess godliness but know nothing of God's salvation. An example would be the Inquisition.

The unthinking rabble and the unmerciful religious hierarchy were unwittingly fulfilling that word in Isaiah 53:3 which foretold of the Saviour — "He is despised and rejected of men; a man of sorrows, and acquainted with grief: and we hid as it were our faces from him; he was despised, and we esteemed him not." They did not realize nor did they care to know that the prophecy went on to say: "Surely he hath borne our griefs, and carried our sorrows: yet we did esteem him stricken, smitten of God, and afflicted. But he was wounded for our transgressions, he was bruised for our iniquities: the chastisement of our peace was upon him; and with his stripes we are healed" (Isaiah 53:4, 5).

God the Father was *there*. He was not seen by those present nor does the account contain any statement about His presence. However, on the day of Pentecost, Peter, by the enlightenment of the Holy Spirit, declared to the multitude, many of whom had been at Calvary:

> Ye men of Israel, hear these words; Jesus of Nazareth, a man approved of God among you by miracles and wonders and signs, which God did by him in the midst of you, as ye yourselves also know: Him, being delivered by the determinate counsel and foreknowledge of God, ye have taken, and by wicked hands have crucified and slain . . . (Acts 2:22, 23).

It was "by the determinate counsel and foreknowledge of God" that the Lamb of God was fulfilling all the Old Testament ceremonial sacrifices and dying in the sinner's place. Therefore the Scripture says: "He that spared not his own Son, but delivered him up for us all, how shall he not with him also freely give us all things" (Romans 8:32).

The devil and many of his demons were *there*. All down the ages Satan had hated God and mankind and had sought to make impossible the promise of Genesis 3:15 that the Seed of the woman should bruise his head. He had endeavored to have the infant Jesus slain by Herod's sword. Calvary's cross was to be the culmination of his demonic rebellion against Almighty God. The adversary of God and man had boasted, "I will ascend into heaven, I will exalt my throne above the stars of God . . . I will be like the Most High" (Isaiah 14:13, 14), and to accomplish his ends he first of all had to destroy the heir, God the Son Himself.

But it was on that cross that the Saviour conquered decisively and with finality the devil and the demon hordes. The Scriptures teach plainly and pointedly that the Lord Jesus in His death was "blotting out the handwriting of ordinances that was against us, which was contrary to us, and took it out of the way, nailing it to his cross; and having spoiled principalities and powers, he made a shew of them openly, triumphing over them in it" (Colossians 2:14, 15).

In a very real sense every believer in Christ was *there*. By becoming a member of His mystical Body, through faith, we are identified with Him in His death and resurrection. The Word teaches us that

> if we have been planted together in the likeness of his death, we shall be also in the likeness of his resurrection: Knowing this, that our old man is crucified with him, that the body of sin might be destroyed, that henceforth we should not serve sin. For he that is dead is freed from sin. Now if we be dead with Christ, we believe that we shall also live with him: Knowing that Christ being raised from the dead dieth no more; death hath no more dominion over him. For in that he died, he died unto sin once: but in that he liveth, he liveth unto God. Likewise reckon ye also yourselves to be dead indeed unto sin, but alive unto God through Jesus Christ our Lord (Romans 6:5-11).

Made one with Him we died with Him, we arose with Him, and in eternity the theme of our song will be: "Unto him that loved us, and washed us from our sins in his own blood" (Revelation 1:5).

201

The cross is the focal point of history. *There* the love of God was declared and made available to all so that *there* is salvation for all who will believe and receive the Saviour, and likewise *there* is the judgment of God against all who will not receive His mercy.

Trust in the Lord

Blessed is he that is trusting the Lord,
  For the help that he daily needs;
He shall inherit the promised reward,
  If he follow where Jesus leads.

Blessed is he that is trusting the Lord,
  Who doth follow the heav'nly way;
Keeping with patience and hope the path,
  All his steps shall be guarded each day.

Blessed is he whom the Father will aid,
  And the Saviour will e'er befriend;
He shall not fear, and shall not be dismayed,
  For the Lord will his soul defend.

Blessed is he who will keep in the way
  That will upward and onward lead;
Walking by faith in His love ev'ry day,
  Who supplieth his daily need.

— IDA L. REED

33

THEN am I strong

And lest I should be exalted above measure through the abundance of the revelations, there was given to me a thorn in the flesh, the messenger of Satan to buffet me, lest I should be exalted above measure. For this thing I besought the Lord thrice, that it might depart from me. And he said unto me, My grace is sufficient for thee: for my strength is made perfect in weakness. Most gladly therefore will I rather glory in my infirmities, that the power of Christ may rest upon me. Therefore I take pleasure in infirmities, in reproaches, in necessities, in persecutions, in distresses for Christ's sake: for when I am weak, *then* am I strong.   — II Corinthians 12:7-10

For when I am weak, *then* am I strong. — II Corinthians 12:10

THE Christian life is not one of freedom from temptation, but rather a triumph in temptation. It is not marked by the absence of adversity but rather by the awareness of God's abundant grace in the midst of it. It is not without struggle, but it also is not without strength in the very midst of strife.

The Lord never promises immunity from trial and suffering; He assures us, rather, He will go *through* it with us. To "go through" predicts a future, something else to come, a consummation, a "latter end." Such is the encouraging word in Isaiah 43:2: "When thou passest through the waters, I will be with thee; and through the rivers, they shall not overflow thee: when thou walkest through the fire, thou shalt not be burned; neither shall the flame kindle upon thee."

The Christian is to be victorious in spirit during the conflict as well as at its conclusion. His instructions read: "Nay, *in* all these things we are more than conquerors through Him that loved us" (Romans 8:37). It is *in* the tribulation, the distress, the persecution, the famine, the peril, when there is no prospect of human help, that we are to be overcomers. It is *in,* and not *after* the trial that we are to be triumphant. Psalm 112:4 has always been a very helpful Scripture to me. It says, "Unto the upright there ariseth light in the darkness . . ." The light arises in the darkness, not after the gloom has given way to the gladness of brighter circumstances.

It has always been so for God's people. Moses endured the complaining, recrimination and rebellion of his people because with the inner eye of the spirit he saw the invisible One. Gideon learned that his sufficiency was wholly of God and therefore could allow his large army to dwindle away into a mere three hundred stout-hearted men. When beset by enemies far stronger than his armed forces, King Jehoshaphat prayed with both earnestness and objectivity: "O our God, wilt thou not judge them? for we have no might against this great company that cometh against us; neither know we what to do: but our eyes are upon thee" (II Chronicles 20:12). Now listen to the assurance from the Spirit of God: "Ye shall not need to fight in this battle: set yourselves, stand ye still, and see the salvation of the Lord with you, O Judah and Jerusalem: fear not, nor be dismayed; to morrow go out against them: for the Lord will be with you" (II Chronicles 20:17). The battle was won in the king's heart before the army moved forward.

When called into God's service in a day of spiritual declension and darkness, young Jeremiah objected, saying, "Ah, Lord God! behold, I cannot speak: for I am a child" (Jeremiah 1:6). Thereupon God replied:

> Say not, I am a child: for thou shalt go to all that I shall send thee, and whatsoever I command thee thou shalt speak. Be not afraid of their faces: for I am with thee to deliver thee, saith the Lord. . . .

> For, behold, I have made thee this day a defenced city, and an iron pillar, and brasen walls against the whole land, against the kings of Judah, against the princes thereof, against the priests thereof, and against the people of the land. And they shall fight against thee; but they shall not prevail against thee; for I am with thee, saith the LORD, to deliver thee (Jeremiah 1:7, 8, 18, 19).

Many times in Jeremiah's ministry it must have seemed that God's promise could not possibly come true, but the prophet was "more than conqueror" in his faithful God.

The honor roll of God's men and women of faith contains this citation: "Who through faith subdued kingdoms, wrought righteousness, obtained promises, stopped the mouths of lions, quenched the violence of fire, escaped the edge of the sword, out of weakness were made strong . . ." (Hebrews 11:33, 34). They learned by experience, as did the Apostle Paul, that "when I am weak then am I strong."

The Christian life is a warfare, and it means triumph during the testing until the inward victory becomes outer — an utter overcoming of the enemy described as "having done all to stand." It is light in the darkness and not after it has disappeared. It is song in the midst of sorrow, and peace in pain. It is quietness of heart when all round about is confusion and hurry. It is keeping one's head, as Kipling observed, when others are losing theirs and blaming it on you. It is the courage of convictions in the face of unmitigated criticism and merciless misrepresentation. It is the gladness of grace when all about are grumbling and gloomy. It is patience under pressure and praise amidst impossibilities.

There is a passage in John Bunyan's autobiography entitled *Grace Abounding to the Greatest of Sinners* at which I have paused often for enlightenment and encouragement. Out of long experience in Bedford's jail where he was imprisoned for preaching the Gospel, Bunyan wrote:

> I never had in all my life so great an inlet into the word of God as now: those Scriptures that I saw nothing in before were made in this place and state to shine upon me; Jesus Christ also was never more real and apparent than now — here I have seen and felt him indeed: O that word, "We have not preached unto you cunningly devised fables," and that, "God raised Christ up from the dead, and gave him

glory, that our faith and hope might be in God," were blessed words unto me in this imprisoned condition (II Peter 1:16; I Peter 1:21). These three or four Scriptures also have been great refreshments in this condition to me — John 14:1-4; 16:33; Colossians 3:3, 4; Hebrews 12:22-24. So that sometimes when I have enjoyed the savour of them I have been able to laugh at destruction, and to fear neither the horse nor his rider.

I never knew what it was for God to stand by me at all times, and at every offer of Satan to afflict me, as I have found him since I came in hither; for, lo! as fears have presented themselves, so have supports and encouragements; yea, when I have started, even as it were at nothing else but my shadow, yet God, as being very tender of me, hath not suffered me to be molested, but would with one Scripture or another strengthen me against all; insomuch that I have often said, were it lawful I could pray for greater trouble for the greater comfort's sake. (Ecclesiastes 7:14; II Corinthians 1:5.)

This is learning firsthand and with finality that "when I am weak, *then* am I strong" because of the Strong Son of God.

My Times Are in Thy Hand

"My times are in Thy hand":
  My God, I wish them there;
My life, my friends, my soul — I leave
  Entirely to Thy care.

"My times are in Thy hand,"
  Whatever they may be;
Pleasing or painful, dark or bright,
  As best may seem to Thee.

"My times are in Thy hand";
  Why should I doubt or fear?
My Father's hand will never cause
  His child a needless tear.

"My times are in Thy hand,"
  Jesus, the crucified!
The hand my cruel sins had pierced,
  Is now my guard and guide.

— W. F. LLOYD

34

THEN sudden destruction cometh

But of the times and the seasons, brethren, ye have no need that I write unto you. For yourselves know perfectly that the day of the Lord so cometh as a thief in the night. For when they shall say, Peace and safety; then sudden destruction cometh upon them, as travail upon a woman with child; and they shall not escape. But ye, brethren, are not in darkness, that that day should overtake you as a thief. Ye are all the children of light, and the children of the day: we are not of the night, nor of darkness. Therefore let us not sleep, as do others; but let us watch and be sober. For they that sleep sleep in the night; and they that be drunken are drunken in the night. But let us, who are of the day, be sober, putting on the breastplate of faith and love; and for an helmet, the hope of salvation. For God hath not appointed us to wrath, but to obtain salvation by our Lord Jesus Christ, Who died for us, that, whether we wake or sleep, we should live together with him. Wherefore comfort yourselves together, and edify one another even as also ye do.   — I Thessalonians 5:1-11

For when they shall say, Peace and safety; *then* sudden destruction cometh upon them . . .   I Thessalonians 5:3

HISTORY, as we know it, will have an ending just as it had a beginning. Human history began with the creation of mankind in the image of God and will conclude at the Second Coming of Christ. Human history does not date from the ageless past, as alleged by evolutionists, nor is it to continue for some billions of years until the light and heat of the sun have disappeared with the deterioration of solar energy. History does not move in great cycles returning periodically to the point of beginning, as alleged by some Greek philosophers of long ago whose philosophy of history was based upon the polytheism of ancient Attica. History is moving in a straight line toward its climax and conclusion which, in the sacred Scriptures, is defined as the ever-imminent, impending Coming of Christ.

There have always been disbelievers in any divine oversight and direction to history, and our age is no exception in that regard. The Bible plainly states that this unbelief will continue and even increase: "Know this first, that there shall come in the last days scoffers, walking after their own lusts, and saying, Where is the promise of his coming? for since the fathers fell asleep, all things continue as they were from the beginning of the creation" (II Peter 3:3, 4). That same Scripture then refers to the destruction of the earth by water sometime in the past and predicts that "the heavens and the earth, which are now, by the same word are kept in store, reserved unto fire against the day of judgment and perdition of ungodly men" (II Peter 3:7).

Nowhere in Scripture is there any definite statement as to the date of that Coming. All down the centuries there have been those who have ignored the plain statement by the Saviour that

> of that day and hour knoweth no man, no, not the angels of heaven, but my Father only. But as the days of Noe were, so shall also the coming of the Son of man be. For as in the days that were before the flood they were eating and drinking, marrying and giving in marriage, until the day that Noe entered in the ark, and knew not until the flood came, and took them all away; so shall also the coming of the Son of man be (Matthew 24:36-39).

More than a century ago the followers of William Miller, clad in white, assembled on hilltops to await the coming of Christ on a given day. And in this century there were teachers of prophecy who were positive that Benito Mussolini, the Fascist dictator of Italy (who was hanged by his heels in 1945) was the "man of dark countenance" foretold in the book of Daniel and therefore the Antichrist.

We are taught to love the appearing of the Lord Jesus and not to speculate about the Antichrist, to be ready at any moment, for no one knows the time of the Lord's appearing.

The Scriptures, Old Testament and New, have many references to the Second Coming of Christ, many more in fact than to His first coming in Bethlehem. Some portions like Isaiah 11 definitely predict a golden age to come, which we understand to be the millennium which will follow the return of Christ. Romans 8:19-23 is one of the New Testament statements relating to the millennial age. The *Amplified* Version translates this portion:

> For (even the whole) creation (all nature) waits expectantly and longs earnestly for God's sons to be made known — waits for the revealing, the disclosing of their sonship. For the creation (nature) was subjected to frailty — to futility, condemned to frustration — not because of some intentional fault on its part, but by the will of Him Who so subjected it. [Yet] with the hope [Ecclesiastes 1:2.] That nature (creation) itself will be set free from its bondage to decay and corruption [and gain an entrance] into the glorious freedom of God's children. We know that the whole creation (of irrational creatures) has been moaning together in the pains of labor until now. [Jeremiah 12:4, 11.] And not only the creation, but we ourselves too, who have and enjoy the first fruits of the (Holy) Spirit — a foretaste of the blissful things to come — groan inwardly as we wait for the redemption of our bodies [from sensuality and the grave, which will reveal] our adoption (our manifestation as God's sons).

Other Old Testament portions, like Isaiah 2 and Micah 4, predict a warless age when men shall beat their swords into plowshares and their spears into pruning hooks because the Sovereign of the universe is here in person. There are many other substantiating portions, some of which are clearly defined in relation to the coming of Christ and others which are assumed by inference so to be.

No one can read the life and teachings of the Lord Jesus as recorded in the four gospels without seeing that the Second Coming is often mentioned. The reference may appear to be just a detail, as for example in Matthew 13:39, which records the Saviour's words: ". . . the harvest is the end of the world [literally, the end of the age]; and the reapers are the angels." In Matthew 28:20 Jesus gave assurance of His presence with His own "even unto the end of the world [age]." Portions such as Matthew 24, Mark 13, Luke 12, 17 and 21 all teach clearly the fact of His return to this earth in judgment after His absence for a time.

On the occasion of the healing of the lame man at the Beautiful Gate, the Apostle Peter gave this exhortation:

> Repent ye therefore, and be converted, that your sins may be blotted out, when the times of refreshing shall come from the presence of the Lord; and he shall send Jesus Christ, which before was preached unto you; whom the heaven must receive until the times of restitution of all things, which God hath spoken by the mouth of all his holy prophets since the world began (Acts 3:19-21).

At a later time he wrote, by inspiration of the Holy Spirit, that "the end of all things is at hand: be ye therefore sober, and watch unto prayer" (I Peter 4:7).

Among Peter's last words, recorded in sacred writ (II Peter 3:10-14), is a further statement about the Second Coming:

> But the day of the Lord will come as a thief in the night; in the which the heavens shall pass away with a great noise, and the elements shall melt with fervent heat, the earth also and the works that are therein shall be burned up. Seeing then that all these things shall be dissolved, what manner of persons ought ye to be in all holy conversation and godliness, looking for and hasting unto the coming of the day of God, wherein the heavens being on fire shall be dissolved, and the elements shall melt with fervent heat? Nevertheless we, according to his promise, look for new heavens and a new earth, wherein dwelleth righteousness. Wherefore, beloved, seeing that ye look for such things, be diligent that ye may be found of him in peace, without spot, and blameless.

In the letters of Paul there are many references to our Lord's coming again. In I Thessalonians 4 is the wonderful portion that has comforted God's people through the ages with the prospect of reunion with loved ones dead in Christ, and with the Saviour. John the beloved apostle, likewise writing under inspiration of the Holy Spirit, gives teaching such as I John 3:2, 3: "Beloved, now are we the sons of God, and it doth not yet appear what we shall be: but we know that, when he shall appear, we shall be like him; for we shall see him as he is. And every man that hath this hope in him purifieth himself, even as he is pure."

But when will be the time of His coming? The date is never stated, but the times are described. One of these indications is in the Scripture text for this meditation: "For when they shall say peace and safety; then sudden destruction cometh upon them, as travail upon a woman with child; and they shall not escape" (v. 3).

The figure of speech is graphic. The labor pains that precede the birth of a child begin and conclude suddenly, and in the meantime they are periodic with increasing intensity. That principle has always been true of God's judgments in the earth. There was long warning in the day of Noah before the flood came, but finally it arrived with suddenness. There were protracted periods of devastating siege before Jerusalem was captured by the Chaldeans in the days of the prophet Jeremiah. The same was true of that city in its capture and destruction by the Romans in the year A.D. 70. The principle in miniature is evident in the life of the impenitent who have repeated warning before the hour of death.

The coming of Christ will be as sudden as the onset of travail for the expectant mother, or like the coming of the thief in the night. It will be so unexpected that there will not be a moment in which to make preparation. The Saviour spoke plainly:

I tell you, in that night there shall be two men in one bed; the one shall be taken, and the other shall be left. Two women shall be grinding together; the one shall be taken, and the other left. Two men shall be in the field; the one shall be taken, and the other left (Luke 17:34-36).

The sudden destruction attending the Second Coming of the Saviour refers to the unbelievers, the impenitent, the unprepared. Another Scripture describes that destruction, which is not annihilation, for the Word does not include that concept. It is dreadful to contemplate. It states:

And to you who are troubled rest with us, when the Lord Jesus shall be revealed from heaven with his mighty angels, in flaming fire taking vengeance on them that know not God, and that obey not the gospel of our Lord Jesus Christ: Who shall be punished with everlasting destruction from the presence of the Lord, and from the glory of his power; when he shall come to be glorified in his saints, and to be admired in all them that believe (because our testimony among you was believed) in that day (II Thessalonians 1:7-10).

That which will be destruction to sinners will be delight to the saints of God, who will be delivered at the appearing of their Lord and Saviour Jesus Christ. For every believer the promise of that coming is precious, as stated in John 14:2, 3 — "In my Father's house are many mansions: if it were not so, I would have told you. I go to prepare a place for you. And if I go and prepare a place for you, I will come again, and receive you unto myself; that where I am, there ye may be also."

The children of light are not to be in darkness so that the day of the Lord's coming overtake them as a thief. They are to be watchful and waiting, vigilant and victorious in spirit, with love for His appearing. For them there is the solemn warning against materialism and unmindfulness of the Lord's coming, even as our Lord taught:

> Take heed to yourselves, lest at any time your hearts be overcharged with surfeiting, and drunkenness, and cares of this life, and so that day come upon you unawares. For as a snare shall it come on all them that dwell on the face of the whole earth. Watch ye therefore, and pray always, that ye may be accounted worthy to escape all these things that shall come to pass, and to stand before the Son of man (Luke 21:34-36).

All this shall come to pass when men are saying, perhaps wistfully, perhaps in self-confidence: Peace and safety! Even now men are saying, Peace, Peace; but it is obvious to anyone that there is no peace. There is abroad in the earth the promise of a false millennium. Satan, posing as an angel of light, is presenting a false messiah by the name of Karl Marx and a pseudo-millennium as the Marxist "classless society," which is the ultimate of history according to that communist persuasion. There are those who believe that mankind itself will create peace and safety when communism prevails over the earth.

The Third Communist International in its *Blueprint for World Conquest* stated:

> The ultimate aim of the Communist International is to replace world capitalist economy by a world system of communism. Communist Society, the basis for which has been prepared by the whole course

of historical development, is mankind's only way out, for it alone can abolish the contradictions of the capitalist system which threatens to degrade and destroy the human race. Communist Society will abolish the class division of society, i.e., simultaneously with the abolition of anarchy in production, it will abolish all forces of exploitation, and oppression of man by man. Society will no longer consist of antagonistic classes in conflict with each other, but will represent a united commonwealth of labor. For the first time in its history mankind will take its fate into its own hands (Blueprint for World Conquest as outlined by The Communist International). (Washington: *Human Events,* 1946, p. 179.)

There is no assurance that communism will continue to increase for certainly it is against nature as well as against God. It may continue indefinitely to gender strife and confusion in the world rather than peace and safety. Whatever it may mean, the Scriptures themselves are clear that there will be the day when mankind is confident that it controls its own destiny in security; and then comes sudden destruction of the world system and of sinners at the coming again of the Son of Man.

For the unsaved the word is, "Be ye also ready, for the coming of the Lord draweth nigh." For God's people the final word is to be aware of the time,

that now it is high time to awake out of sleep: for now is our salvation nearer than when we believed. The night is far spent, the day is at hand: let us therefore cast off the works of darkness, and let us put on the armour of light. Let us walk honestly, as in the day; not in rioting and drunkenness, not in chambering and wantonness, not in strife and envying. But put ye on the Lord Jesus Christ, and make not provision for the flesh, to fulfil the lusts thereof (Romans 13: 11-14).

35

No night THERE

And the city had no need of the sun, neither of the moon, to shine in it: for the glory of God did lighten it, and the Lamb is the light thereof. And the nations of them which are saved shall walk in the light of it: and the kings of the earth do bring their glory and honour into it. And the gates of it shall not be shut at all by day: for there shall be no night *there*. And they shall bring the glory and honour of the nations into it. . . . And there shall be no more curse: but the throne of God and of the Lamb shall be in it; and his servants shall serve him: And they shall see his face; and his name shall be in their foreheads. And there shall be no night there; and they need no candle, neither light of the sun; for the Lord God giveth them light: and they shall reign for ever and ever. And he said unto me, These sayings are faithful and true: and the Lord God of the holy prophets sent his angel to shew unto his servants the things which must shortly be done. Behold, I come quickly: blessed is he that keepeth the sayings of the prophecy of this book.   — Revelation 21:23-26; 22:3-7

For there shall be no night *there*.   — Revelation 21:25

THERE is no night there.

We are all familiar with day and night. Because of the rotation of the earth from west to east the sun appears to sink beyond the western horizon, and the night comes. The Most

219

High made provision for day and night in the creation when He said: "Let there be lights in the firmament of the heaven to divide the day from the night; and let them be for signs, and for seasons, and for days, and years." (Genesis 1:14).

In a metaphorical sense the night represents a season of sorrow and loss, of grief and pain, of utter discouragement and disillusionment, of human helplessness and hopelessness. The patriarch Job spoke of the night in concepts both literal and figurative when in his groaning he sighed: "When I lie down, I say, When shall I arise, and the night be gone? and I am full of tossings to and fro unto the dawning of the day" (Job 7:4).

It was Elihu who sought to assure the bewildered Job that God gives songs in the night (Job 35:10). The psalmist, David, was aware of God's goodness in times of depression or danger and therefore he could say: "Sing unto the Lord, O ye saints of his, and give thanks at the remembrance of his holiness. For his anger endureth but a moment; in his favour is life: weeping may endure for a night, but joy cometh in the morning" (Psalm 30:4, 5).

The present age is likened in the Scriptures to the night. "Knowing the time," states Romans 13:11, 12, "that now it is high time to awake out of sleep: for now is our salvation nearer than when we believed. The night is far spent, the day is at hand: let us therefore cast off the works of darkness, and let us put on the armour of light."

In the darkness and chaos of the present time all creation groans in the bondage of corruption. And we wait with increasing expectation for the dawn, for when Jesus the Light of the world returns, then earth's long night will be over.

There is no night *there!* Twice is that assurance stated in the Scripture. What that will mean in its entirety to the redeemed we cannot know or fully comprehend. The Word in I Corinthians 2:9, 10 tells us:

> Eye hath not seen, nor ear heard, neither have entered into the heart of man, the things which God hath prepared for them that love him. But God hath revealed them unto us by his Spirit: for the Spirit searchest all things, yea, the deep things of God.

In the closing chapters of the Apocalypse we have the revelation of what is to be *there*. We believe every word of it even though only dimly can we now understand it.

Heaven is a place as well as a state for the people of God. We are told there is a city, a place prepared as promised by the Saviour. The first thing said of that city is that God's people shall be in His presence forever. The Word declares: "And I heard a great voice out of heaven saying, Behold, the tabernacle of God is with men, and he will dwell with them, and they shall be his people, and God himself shall be with them, and be their God" (Revelation 21:3).

Because of that Presence all that is associated with earth's night is in the past. Again the Word:

> And God shall wipe away all tears from their eyes; and there shall be no more death, neither sorrow, nor crying, neither shall there be any more pain: for the former things are passed away. And he that sat upon the throne said, Behold, I make all things new. And he said unto me, Write: for these words are true and faithful (Revelation 21:4, 5).

All things new — who can grasp that concept? No tears because of our sins and failures, nor because of the loss of loved ones, no death with its separation and sorrow, not even any pain!

The city itself is described in considerable detail (21:1-21), and concludes with the observation that there is "no temple therein," because it is all worship. "The Lord God Almighty and the Lamb are the temple of it" (v. 22).

Furthermore, because of God's presence there is no need of sun nor of moon to shine in it because "the Lamb is the light thereof." With Him and in His presence there can be no night, physical or figurative.

Man's attempts at describing that city of light as a rule fall far short of what our heart perceives in these Scriptures. John Bunyan had by far the best comprehension and wrote the most eloquent expression of that city and its inhabitants in his *Pilgrim's Progress*. Let us turn to that book and in imagination, sit beside God's servant in the gloomy prison cell in Bedford, and with him behold the entrance of Christian and Hopeful into that city. After the two pilgrims passed through the river of death they saw "two shining men again, who there waited for them." They saluted Christian and Hopeful, saying:

"We are ministering spirits, sent forth to minister for those that shall be heirs of salvation." Thus they went along towards the gate. Now you must note, that the city stood upon a mighty hill; but the pilgrims went up that hill with ease, because they had these two men to lead them up by the arms: they had likewise left their mortal garments behind them in the river; for though they went in with them, they came out without them. They therefore went up here with much agility and speed, though the foundation upon which the city was framed was higher than the clouds; they therefore went up through the region of the air, sweetly talking as they went, being comforted because they safely got over the river, and had such glorious companions to attend them.

The talk that they had with the shining ones was about the glory of the place; who told them that the beauty and glory of it was inexpressible. There, said they, is "Mount Sion, the heavenly Jerusalem, the innumerable company of angels, and the spirits of just men made perfect" (Hebrews 12:22-24). . . . The men then asked, "What must we do in the holy place?" To whom it was answered, "You must there receive the comfort of all your toil, and have joy for all your sorrow; you must reap what you have sown, even the fruit of all your prayers, and tears, and sufferings for the King by the way" (Galatians 6:8). "In that place you must wear crowns of gold, and enjoy the perpetual sight and vision of the Holy One; for 'there you shall see him as he is'" (I John 3:2). "There also you shall serve Him continually with praise, with shouting and thanksgiving, whom you desired to serve in the world, though with much difficulty, because of the infirmity of your flesh. There your eyes shall be delighted with seeing, and your ears with hearing the pleasant voice of the Mighty One. There you shall enjoy your friends again that are gone thither before you; and there you shall with joy receive even every one that follows into the holy place after you."

Now, while they were thus drawing towards the gate, behold a company of the heavenly host came out to meet them: to whom it was said by the other two shining ones, "These are the men that have loved our Lord when they were in the world, and that have left all for his holy name; and he hath sent us to fetch them, and we have brought them thus far on their desired journey, that they may go in and look their Redeemer in the face with joy." Then the heavenly host gave a great shout, saying, "Blessed are they that are called to the marriage supper of the Lamb" (Revelation 19:9). There came out also at this time to meet them several of the King's trumpeters, clothed in white and shining raiment, who, with melodious noises

222

and loud, made even the heavens to echo with their sound. These trumpeters saluted Christian and his fellow with ten thousand welcomes from the world; and this they did with shouting and sound of trumpet.

And now were these two men, as it were, in heaven, before they came to it, being swallowed up with the sight of angels, and with hearing of their melodious notes. Here also they had the city itself in view; and they thought they heard all the bells therein to ring, to welcome them thereto. But above all, the warm and joyful thoughts that they had about their own dwelling there with such company, and that forever and ever; oh, by what tongue or pen can their glorious joy be expressed! Thus they came up to the gate.

Now when they were come up to the gate, there was written over it, in letters of gold, "Blessed are they that do his commandments, that they may have right to the tree of life, and may enter in through the gates into the city."

Now I saw in my dream, that these two men went in at the gate; and lo, as they entered, they were transfigured; and they had raiment put on that shone like gold. There were also that met them with harps and crowns, and gave them to them; the harps to praise withal, and the crowns in token of honour. Then I heard in my dream, that all the bells in the city rang again for joy, and that it was said to them,

"Enter ye into the joy of your Lord."

I also heard the men themselves, that they sang with a loud voice, saying,

"Blessing, and Honour, and Glory, and Power, be unto him that sitteth upon the throne, and unto the Lamb, forever and ever."

Now, just as the gates were opened to let in the men, I looked in after them, and behold the city shone like the sun; the streets also were paved with gold; and in them walked many men, with crowns upon their heads, palms in their hands, and golden harps, to sing praises withal.

There were also of them that had wings, and they answered one another without intermission, saying, "Holy, holy, holy is the Lord." And after that they shut up the gates: which, when I had seen, I wished myself among them.

From Bunyan we turn back to Scripture and begin to understand perhaps a little better than before what is written therein:

And there shall be no more curse: but the throne of God and of the Lamb shall be in it; and his servants shall serve him: And they shall see his face; and his name shall be in their foreheads. And there shall be no night there; and they need no candle, neither light of the sun; for the Lord God giveth them light: and they shall reign for ever and ever (22:3-5).